THE PHILOSOPHY OF FIRE

(LOVE, GOD)

SYMBOL OF FIRE

BY DR. R. SWINBURNE CLYMER

Author of " The Rosicrucians; their teachings," "Ancient Mystic Oriental Masonry", "True Spiritualism," "Divine Alchemy." etc.

REVISED EDITION.   COPYRIGHTED.

PUBLISHED BY
THE PHILOSOPHICAL PUBLISHING CO.
ALLENTOWN, PA.

DEDICATION

To her who must be NAMELESS but who has so faithfully stood by me in all my sorrow and trouble and who is still the Guiding Spirit of my work, and also, to all such who are working for the good of ALL and the Universal Brotherhood of Man, is this work Lovingly dedicated.

BY THE AUTHOR.

PREFACE.

(*Second and Enlarged Edition.*)

When, less than a year ago, the first edition of the "Philosophy of Fire" was issued, we had feared that the whole edition could never be sold, knowing how slowly books of this nature sell. What then was our surprise when we found that some of those who first subscribed to the book would order as many as six copies to present to their friends, and what still more surprised us was that many of the Occult Orders would order many copies for their members. And now, all within one short year, the whole edition of the book is sold, and not a single letter of criticism has been received except in a few instances where the purchasers thought the appearance could be better. Nor can we blame them for it was far from perfect although we had ordered, and been promised, the best possible work.

Now that the opportunity is presented to issue another edition, I have taken time to enlarge the work and have added a large chapter on the Rosicrucian Fire-Philosophy, mainly from the work "The Rosicrucians, their Rites and Mysteries" by Hargrave Jennings, and which is a work that is not to be had at the present time, and therefore gives greater value to the present edition of this work.

1 I

With this addition to the work and the far more perfect workmanship, we believe that it will sell even faster than did the first edition, and, from the way orders are coming in at this present time, we have no doubt but that another edition will be needed within the year. *For all this we beg to thank our subscribers and to assure them that we more than appreciate their effort to spread this great Doctrine, the fundamental principle of All Religion.*

R. SWINBURNE CLYMER.

ALLENTOWN, PA., FEBRUARY 10, 1907.

INTRODUCTION.

" There is nothing new under the sun "

Thus has a wise man said in the long ago and
Marie Corelli, the most justly famous authoress of
the present day, in her beautiful book, "A Romance
of Two Worlds," says: "Yours? Why, what can
you call your own? Every talent you have, every
breath you draw, every drop of blood flowing in
your veins, is lent to you only; you must pay it all
back. And as far as the arts go, it is a bad sign of
poet, painter, or musician, who is arrogant enough
to call his work his own. It never was his and
never will be. It is planned by a higher intelligence than his, only he happens to be the hired laborer chosen to carry out the conception; a sort of
mechanic in whom boastfulness looks absurd; as
absurd as if one of the stone-masons working at
the cornice of a cathedral were to vaunt himself as
the designer of the whole edifice. And when a
work, any work, is completed, it passes out of the
laborer's hands; it belongs to the age and the people for whom it was accomplished, and, if deserving,
goes on belonging to the future ages and future
peoples." So with the book that is now being
placed before the reader, I wish him to remember
that it is not my own. I have taken the works of

7

many of those before me and have tried to choose
therefrom such material as has appealed to me. I
have taken this material and have tried to arrange
it so as to form one harmonious whole. I wish the
reader to understand that even this material was
not original with the authors from whom I quote.
For instance, the Secret Doctrine has come down
to us from the Temples of Atlantis and no one is
able to tell us how long ago that may have been.
The Ancient Mysteries also were handed down by
Initiate to Initiate from that same time. The question may well be asked by the reader why it is necessary to again repeat the things that have already
been written? It is a fair question and deserves a
fair answer. *It is for the reason that these authors
stated the facts here set forth, in the negative form. It
is my desire to state that they are positive facts. Facts
that can be verified by "Him who truly seeks in earnest."*
In many cases, these authors state the things that
they had read, and, not belonging to any Fraternity
that can give them the positive facts, and not having
access to the secret records, are unable to say that
these things are true. Knowing the interest taken
in the Higher Science, Occultism, Mysticism and
the True Initiation, and having the records at my
command which prove that the things herein written are true, is my excuse for the compilation of
the presest work. I do not wish to be accused of
plagiarism and therefore the foregoing. I do not
claim that a single line in this book is my own. I
claim nothing, but give the credit to those who have
gone before me. If you find anything original,

give the credit to those who have taught me and not
to me. By doing this, you will not give me credit
for that which does not belong to me. One thing I
wish the truly interested reader to remember—
whatever is herein written is absolutely true and
if you are willing to so change your life as to be
worthy, there are those who are ever ready to teach
you and show you the Path that leads to Initiation
— *The finding of the Christ.*

History informs us that: "As soon as mankind
recognized the relation between themselves and a
Creator, and acknowledged moral responsibility to a
Supreme Moral Government, then Religion became
a pertinent fact, and systems of religion were introduced, whereby, in an objective form, their subjec-
ivity could be outwardly made manifest.

"These systems are divided into monotheism and
Polytheism: the latter includes Dualism and Trithe-
ism. The lowest grade of Polytheism is Fetichism,
or idolatry, which teaches the worship of inanimate
nature, stocks and stones, and the work of the hands
of men. Next is Pyrolatry, or worship of Fire; and
Sabæism, worship of the sun.

"The first step of each Master or Reformer was
to receive a mission and revelation from some God:
thus—Amasis and Mneves, Lawgivers of the Egyptians, received their laws from Mercury (Thoth);
Zoroaster of the Bactrians, and Zamolxis, lawgiver
of the Getes, from Vesta; Zathraustes, of the Arm-
aspi, from a good Spirit or Genius: and all progaged
the doctrine of the "Law of Karma." There is no
doubt but that all of them were Initiates of the

Secret Orders then existing and which Orders taught the Secret Doctrine and Ancient Mysteries —as well as the Mystery of the Fire. That this is true will be shown farther on.

Rhadamanthus and Minos, lawgivers of Crete, and Lycaon of Arcadia, had intercourse with Jupiter; Triptolemus of Athens was inspired by Ceres, Pythagoras and Zaleucus, for the Crotonians and Locrians, ascribed their institutions to Minerva, Lycurgus of Sparta acted by direction of Apollo, and Romulus and Numa of Rome put themselves under the guidance of Consus and the goddess Egeria.

The first Chinese monarch was called "Fag-Four" —"The Son of Heaven." Tuesco, the founder of the German nations, was sent to reduce mankind from their savage and bestial life to one of order and society, as appears from his name, which signifies the "interpreter of the gods." Thor and Ogin, the lawgivers of the Western Goths, laid claim to inspiration and to divinity, and they have given the names to two of the days of the week.

Plato makes legislation to have been derived from God, and the constant epithets to kings in Homer are *Dio-geneis*, "born of the gods," and *Dio-trepheis*, "bred or or tutored by the gods." When true Initiation is once understood by scholars they will no longer deny that man can be taught by God or by the Supreme Intelligence, for such a thing is possible, and Divine Revelations to man or to the mind and soul of man, is not so hard or impossible a thing. That these Masters and Reformers received their instructions direct there is no doubt. Man *can* come into direct communication with his God if he is willing to live such a life as will make this possible. In the following work, both proofs of this fact and instructions are given. No one may say that he did not know.

Plutarch, in "Isis and Osiris," says: "It was a most Ancient opinion, derived as well by lawgivers as divines, that the world was not made by chance, neither did one cause govern all things without opposition."

This is the doctrine of Zoroaster, in which were taught two opposite principles by which the world was governed.

The first Religion or Mysteries were those of Atlantis and known as the Hermetic Philosophy. Later, we have the Oriental Mysteries of Isis and Osiris in Egypt. These Mysteries are the same as the Hermetic Philosophy of Atlantis and are but known under another name. The study of the Mysteries of Isis and Osiris will prove to the student that this was a pure Fire Philosophy and this is proven in the pages that are to follow.

Zoroaster brought these Mysteries into Persia; Cadmus and Inachus, into Greece at large, Orpheus, into Thrace, Melampsus, into Athens.

As these Ancient,—"Atlantian Mysteries"— they should be called,—were to Isis and Osiris in Egypt; so they were to Mythras in Asia; in Samothrace, to the Mother of the Gods; in Bœotia to Bacchus; in Cyprus to Venus; in Crete to Jupiter; in Athens to Ceres and Proserpine; in Amphura to

Castor and Pollux; in Lamnos to Vulcan. The most noted of these were the Orphic, Bacchic, Eleusinian, Samothracian, Cabiric, and Mithriac. It was agreed by Origen and Celsus that the Mysteries taught the future life, the Law of Karma, and the Law of Reincarnation. It was taught that the Initiated would be happier than other mortals because they lived so in this world as to learn in the present incarnation what it would take the profane many incarnations to learn. Plato taught that it was the design of Initiation to restore the soul to that state from whence all fell, as from its native seat of perfection. And Epictetus taught that: "Thus the Mysteries become useful, thus we seize the true spirit of them, when we begin to apprehend that everything therein was instituted by the ancients for instruction and amendment of life."

All persons who were candidates for Initiation into any of these Mysteries were required to produce evidence of their fitness by due inquiry into their previous life and character. The Eleusinian stood open to none who did not approach the Gods with a pure and holy worship, which was originally an indispensible condition observed in common in all the Mysteries, and instituted by Bacchus or Osiris, himself who initiated none but virtuous and pious men, and it was required to have a prepared purity of mind and disposition, as previously ordered in the sacrifices, or in prayers, in approaching the Mysteries.

It was Max Muller who wrote that: "In the language of mankind, in which everything *new is old,* and everything *old is new*, an inexhaustible mine has been discovered for researches of this kind. Language still bears the impress of the *earliest* thoughts of man; obliterated, it may be, buried under new thoughts, yet here and there still recoverable in their sharp original outline. The growth of language is continuous, and by continuing our researches backward from the most modern to the most ancient strata, the very elements and roots of human speech have been reached, and with them the elements and roots of human thought. What lies beyond the beginnings of language, however interesting it may be to the physiologist, does not yet belong to the history of man, in the true and original sense of that word. *Man* means the *thinker*, and the first manifestation of thought is speech.

"But more surprising than the continuity of the growth of language is the continuity in the growth of religion. Of religion, as of language, it may be said that in it *everything new is old*, and *everything old is new, and that there has been no entirely new religion since the beginning of the world. The elements and roots of religion were there as far back as we can trace the history of man*, and the history of religion, like the history of language, shows us throughout a succession of *new combinations of the same radical elements*. An Intuition of God, a sense of human weakness and dependence, a belief in the divine government of the world, a distinction between good and evil, and a hope for a better life—these are some of the radical elements of all religions. Though sometimes hidden, they rise again and again to the surface. Though frequently distorted, they tend again and again to their perfect form, though always under another name.

St. Augustine himself, in accordance with this idea, said: "What is now called the Christian religion has existed among the ancients, and was not absent from the beginning of the human race, until Christ came in the flesh, from which time the religion which existed already, began to be called Christian."

As will be proven in the work now before the reader, that the underlying principles in all *true* religions or sects, is the Philosophy of Fire. No matter what the system may be, it is always the same. The very foundation of the Secret Doctrine and the Ancient Doctrine is the Philosophy of Fire —*Love.* In the work before the reader, quotations have been made from the Secret teachings of the greater sects of those Fraternities and Orders who were most instrumental in shaping the Religious beliefs of the people. The only one not so dealt with is Zoroaster.

Before the time of Zoroaster the Persians, like the early Egyptians, worshipped in the open air, long after other nations had constructed temples, as they considered the broad expanse of heavens as the sublime covering of temples devoted to the worship of Deity. Their places of sacrifice were much like those of the northern nations of Europe, composed of circles of upright stones, rough and unhewn. They abominated images, and worshipped the Sun and *Fire,* as *Representatives* of the *Omni-*

present Deity. The Jews, even though they did not belong to the Inner Circle of any Order and thus only followed the exoteric religious ceremonies, were not exempt from the worship of Fire, saying, God appeared in the Cherubim, over the gate of Eden, as a *Flaming Sword*, and to Abraham as *Flame of Fire*, to Moses as a *Fire* in the bush at Horeb, and to the whole assembly of the people at Sinai, when he descended upon the mountain *in Fire.* Moses himself told them that their God was a *Consuming Fire*, which was reechoed more than once, and thence the Jews were weak enough to worship the material substance, in lieu of the *Invisible* and Eternal God. Zoroaster succeeded in persuading them to enclose their sacred fire altars in covered towers, because, being on elevated and exposed hills, the fire was liable to be extinguished by storms. These were circular buildings, covered with domes, having small openings at the top to let out the smoke.

....A Jew entered a Parsee temple and beheld the Sacred Fire. "What," said he to the priest, "do you worship the fire?" "Not the fire," answered the priest, "it *is to us the emblem of the Sun and of his genial heat.*" "Do you then worship the sun as your God?" asked the Jew. "Know ye not that this luminary also is but a work of the Almighty Creator?" "We know it," replied the priest, "but the uncultivated man requires a sensible sign in order to form a conception of the Most High, and is not the sun, the incomprehensible source of light, an image of that invisible being who blesses and preserves all things?" "Do your people, then,"

rejoined the Israelite, "distinguish the type from
the original? They call the sun their God, and,
descending even from this to a baser object, they
kneel before an earthly flame. Ye amuse the outward but blind the inward eye; and while ye hold
to them the earthly, ye draw from them the heavenly Light! Thou shalt not make unto thyself any
image or likeness." "How do you designate the
Supreme Being?" asked the Parsee. "We call him
Jehovah Adonai; that is, the Lord who is, who was,
and who will be," answered the Jew. "Your appel-
lation is grand and sublime," said the Parsee, "but
it is awful too." A Christian then drew nigh and
said, "We call him Father." The Pagan and the
Jew looked at each other and said, "Here is at once
an image and a reality, it is a word of the heart."
Therefore they all raised their eyes to Heaven, and
said, with reverence and Love (Fire), "Our Father,"
and they took each other by the hand, and all three
called one another "brother."

Thus, as has already been stated, the names of
religious systems may be different, but the underlying principle is ever the same. No matter what
exoteric systems of religion may be studied, it will
always be found that God is a "*Consuming Fire.*"
In the teachings of the Ancient Mysteries this is
much more true for the reason that in these Mysteries we are taught what this *living fire* is.

"Ever since the most ancient times *Divine Wisdom* has taught the same doctrines through the
mouths of the wise. Hermes Trismegistus, Confucius and Zoroaster, Buddha and Jesus the Christ,

Plato and Socrates, Saint Martin and Jacob Boeh-men, Theophrastus Paracelsus, Cornelius Agrippa, Shakespeare and Shoppenhauer, P. B. Randolph and Freeman B. Dowd, and others have taught the same truths, more or less complete, because they were *all from the same school of philosophy.* Each of these teachers clothed them in a form most suitable to his own understanding or adapted to the compre-hension of his disciples.

No one can claim that any of these teachings are their own. The Christ said; "The doctrines which I teach are *not my own*, but it is the Truth which teaches them through me. He that teaches his own doctrines and theories speaketh of himself, he is acting under the impulse of earthly ambition and seeketh his own glory and not the glory of God, but he that seeks to glorify—not himself, but God—by giving expression to the truth of which he is conscious, is true, and no evil can be in him. *Live so that you may know the truth; not by external appear-ances and argumentation, but by its own inherent power. Be true, and you will know the truth.*

"The organism of *man*," he said, "resembles a kingdom, its capital is the Mind, and its temple the Soul. In that capital and temple there are many false prophets, as there are in Jerusalem. There are the Pharisees of sophistry and false logic, cre-dulity, and scepticism, and the 'scribes' are the prejudices and erroneous opinions engrafted upon the memory. Do not listen to what these false prophets say, but *listen to the voice of wisdom that speaks in your heart*; for verily I say unto you, the temple, built of speculations which the scribes have erected, will be destroyed, and not one of the dogmas and theories of which it has been constructed will remain, when the day of judgment appears.

"See the truth enters your heart, bearing the palm leaf, the symbol of peace. Let it abide in you, and abide yourself in the truth. There is no other worship acceptable to the Universal God, but to keep his commandments, which he reveals to you through the power of Divine Wisdom, whose voice speaks in your Higher Consciousness. *Love one another;* and as you grow in *unselfish love*, so will you grow in wisdom.

Open your hearts and see the image of the true God *within* them. *He is not to be found in man-made churches; and if any one tells you, Christ is in this church, or he is in that one, do not believe it, but seek for God within your own heart.* Let not the Pharisees and the scribes and the intellectual powers of your own mind mislead you, but listen to the divine voice of Intuition, which speaks at the *center* of your Soul."

Thus, Christ agrees with the fundamental doctrine of the Higher Occult Science taught by our *true* Fraternities of the present day, i. e., that man is the product of his own thoughts, he is that which he makes himself by the way he thinks and acts, for his external form is nothing but an outward symbol of his internal character, modified by the want of plasticity of the gross matter composing his body, for gross matter is not sufficiently plastic to change in form as rapidly as his thoughts. The matter composing the soul is more plastic. If our thoughts are continually low and vulgar, it will become correspondingly degraded, but if we are continually thinking of a high Ideal, our Ideal will take form *within* ourselves. If we are satisfied with a belief in an historical Christ without seeking to cause or enable a Christ to grow *within* ourselves, such a belief will not be merely useless, but it will be an impediment in our way to perfection.

The object of the Higher Occult Science; the Ancient Mysteries; the Secret Doctrines; of *true* Initiation, and of all True Religion is one and the same thing, i. e., to ennoble mankind and to awaken men to a realization of the divinity of the Spirit *within* themselves. Religion in its *theoretical* aspect means a *real* knowledge of the relations which exist between man and the external Source from which his Spirit emanated in the beginning, religion in its *practical* aspect means the union of *man with God,*— a union that cannot be effected through the external interference or permission of a clergyman, but must be effected by the power of the *internal will. There is no real knowledge to be attained by merely learning a theory, there is no real knowledge unless the theory is confirmed by practice.*

This knowledge is acquired neither by the study of theology and philosophy, nor by moralizing. It does not depend on any theoretical information in regard to terrestial or celestial things, nor can spiritual regeneration be attained by leading a virtuous life for fear of the consequences that are likely to follow if we indulge in evil, it can only be acquired by a realization of the truth *within* our own selves. There is nothing to prevent any man from arriving at such a realization, except the lower tendencies of his mortal nature. The process of spiritual regeneration or Initiation, therefore involves a continual battle with the lower self, and unceasing fight between spiritual aspirations and earthly desires, in which the Spirit must gain the victory over Matter.

All the boasted knowledge of the science learned in schools contains no *real* knowledge whatever. It knows nothing of *absolute truth*. It is merely *relative* knowledge, and refers to the relations which external objects bear to each other, and all this knowledge, however useful it may be as long as we live in this world of external illusions and "objective hallucinations," will be entirely useless to us when we enter that state in which those illusions do not exist. *The only true science, which is really useful to us in time and eternity*, in our present condition, not less than in the hereafter, *is the practical knowledge of the regeneration of man.*

If the reader will carefully note all words and sentences that appear in *italics*, he or she will get a far better understanding than could otherwise be had.

Throughout the work, authors quoted from have not been given credit, because it has been my desire to bring forth a work, giving the teachings of the Masters without any interruptions. The authors quoted from are Dr. Paschal Beverly Randolph; Dr. Frantz Hartmann; Dr. J. D. Buck; Hargrave

Jennings; E. Shure, and Dr. P. H. Phelon. Each one of these great teachers has been of as great importance to this work as has the other and equal credit is therefore due to them all.

If the work will be the means of opening the eyes of a few and influence them to try and "find their own Soul," I shall be well satisfied.

THE COMPILER.

The Ancient Mysteries.

"THE belief in a Supreme Power is inherent in every human being; and, so thoroughly interwoven with our nature is this sentiment, that it is impossible for anyone, at any period of life, wholly to divest himself of it.

"When the reflecting man looks around upon all the objects about him, the question naturally arises; 'What has called this world into existence? Why does it exist, and what is its ultimate destiny? Why do I exist, and what will become of me after death? The answers to these questions can only be given by and through a long course of Philosophical investigation. It is these questions that have been the study of the ablest men from the earliest ages, and have given rise to all the various systems of philosophy and religion, which have prevailed in all times, beginning with the first man, and coming down to our own day and generation.

"Of one thing we are certain, the first religion that we have any account of, was far superior to any of those formulated in late centuries *I refer to the Philosophy of the Atlantians.* Theirs was the Pure Fire Philosophy, and not only was it a pure and absolute religion but, at the same time, it gave them the power that true religion should give to its Masters. This the Fire Philosophy of the Atlantians did, and we find, throughout all ages, that those Philosophies, under whatever name, which were founded on the Fire Philosophy, always gave this power to its Initiates. It is only with these Philosophies that I will deal at the present and set forth the history, in compact form, of those systems of Philosophy which worshipped at the Shrine of Fire—Love, and believed this to be all potent. The Philosophers of these systems do *not* worship the Fire as the profane suppose, *but they take Fire as a symbol of that Supreme Power which they believe in and Know to be all powerful and Absolute.*

An author has said: "It is to be presumed that when the minds of men were directed to the subject of the mysterious things of nature which they could not apprehend, they were forced to conceal their ignorance of the ultimate causes for all the phenomena by which they were constantly surrounded, and as constantly called upon to explain, that then, as well as at present, their inventive talents were exercised to conceal their ignorance by systems of terminology." This is not true, the Mysteries did *not* have their origin in such a manner, but rather, because men who were Masters of these Mysteries, knew that it would not do to let the masses know the true meaning of these mysteries and therefore invented symbols and ceremonies in order to teach those who were prepared to know the truth.

"It is, however, conceded that the rites and ceremonies were originally of a pure character and had a tendency to impress the minds of the Initiates with a suitable feeling of awe and reverence for the society, and to benefit their lives in all particulars.

An author who claims to be an authority on the subject, has said: "It is impossible to definitely assert in what country the Mysteries were first introduced. Authors differ very materially upon that question. It is, however, very certain that while there are various changes to be found in the Mysteries of the different nations of the Orient, it is also as certain that there was a great similarity in them all; so much so that we may conclude that either they were all independent copies from a great original system, or that they were propagated one from another, until they were spread over the whole of Asia, Europe, and that part of Africa, peopled from Asia and in constant intercourse therewith. The first wave from that region, now known as Arya Varta, was to the Southeast, and across the great rivers, and into that part of India where they found a people descended from the Turanian families, who had come from the north and northeast. We are informed that, when the Aryans entered the country of India, they carried with them traditions, manners, and customs, and religious ideas, which differed very materially from those possessed by the first inhabitants, who were, no doubt, of Turanian descent."

The author is mistaken in some respects. We *know* absolutely that these mysteries came from Atlantis and that initiation into these Mysteries were first had there. We *know* that in the Temples of Atlantis these Mysteries were first taught to the Neophytes and we *know* that these Mysteries were brought into Asia and India and later, into Egypt, by the Initiates of Atlantis. These things *we* of the Ancient Orders *know* from records now in our hands and hidden in our Sacred and Secret Archives.

The author may well say that it is very certain that while there are various changes to be found in the Mysteries of the different nations of the Orient, it is also as certain that there was a great similarity in them all. Why should they not be alike in their spirit if not entirely in their form since they are all from the same tree? True, changes have been made in both form and name, but this has only been done in order to meet the demands of the time. All Orders founded on the Fire Philosophy come from one great tree, and it has been found that in their spirit they are the same, simply existing under different names, the same as the Order now known as the Rosy Cross was once known as the Paracelsians. It is ever the same Order under a different name. Truly Shakespeare said that a Rose was just as pretty under another name.

The Great Lodge of the Magi, the Adepts, and the Perfect Masters, known and designated also by many other names, has never for a moment ceased to exist; this Lodge has often, though secret and unknown, shaped the course of the very empires and controlled the fate of Nations. France and Napoleon Marleon is a good example, for without the Secret Lodge Napoleon could never have been the mighty Master he was.

These Adepts and Masters, knowing always the

line of least resistance, and when and how to act,
and having always in view only one object, i. e., the
Progress of Humanity and the Universal Brotherhood of Man; despising fame and worldly honors,
and working "without the hope of fee or reward,"
they have concealed their labors, and either influ-
enced those who knew them not to do their work,
or worked through agents pledged to conceal their
very existence.

As these lines are being penned, the news comes
before the world that peace has been declared between Japan and Russia, at the same time, there
comes a letter from one of the truly great on earth
and in which are found these lines: "Looking at
these principle events of today, the concluding of
peace between Japan and Russia, I am given to
know, that the Great White Brotherhood is the *real*
Peace-maker and that President Roosevelt is their
Instrument."

To the public generally, this may be a matter of
little interest or impoi tance, as the character of the
work done must be the sole criterion by which that
work is to be measured.   To the Mystics and Initiates, it should be of interest, as showing what it is
to be, indeed, a Master of the Brotherhood.   It will
reveal to them the meaning and goal of human evolution, and give them the unqualified assurance
that that evolution is being aided *by those who know*,
as it has not been for many centuries.   Such work
has now become possible, because of a cycle of liberality and enlightenment, when the workers are
not likely to be sacrificed by an Inquisition, although

they may be persecuted for their teachings.　Such Masters do exist, and they are truly possessed of profound knowledge, they are ready to help the world, but the world must be *ready* and willing to receive such help, if it is to be benefited by it.　It must not stand ready to destroy both the teachings and its agents.　Guided by a complete Philosophy; armed with a key to Symbolism, and aided by these Masters, the Lost Mysteries may be restored and made to tell their story for the benefit of the coming race.

Mere vulgar curiosity and secrecy alone have never, and will never be the password to the *adytum* of real Initiation.　It will take something more than curiosity to find the Gate to the Path that leads to the true Initiation.　It will take a heart that throbs for the welfare of humanity.　A Love for a Universal Brotherhood of Man.　He alone who seeks Initiation because he desires to help his fellow man can ever hope to be admitted to the Path.

An history of those who have become Initiates would necessarily be tinged with a touch of pathos, on account of the many sorrowful disappointments it would have to record, in the case of earnest souls seeking, with sincerity and in truth, for the "Lost Word of the Master," (the finding of the Christ), only to be publicly executed as malefactors and enemies of State or Church as most of them have been in the past.　None have sought Initiation in Love but that they have found the Path and the Christ. That such organizations and Masters should exist through all time and yet be without a history seems

at first a strange paradox. The enemies of Mysti·
cism and Philosophy will urge this fact as a reason
for rejecting all that is herein contained, ignorant
of the fact that few histories of any people or any
epoch are better founded. Foremost among these
detractors or deniers will be found the bigoted sec·
tarian and the modern materialist. With each of
these, the real genius of Mysticism is in perpetual
conflict. For the first, the universal and unquali·
fied Brotherhood of Man, is a dead letter, for he
believes that only himself and his chosen associates
can be saved. For the second, the materialist, the
recognition of the Divine Principle in Man, and be·
lief in the Immortality of the Soul, will prove an
equal stumbling block. Fortunately, the number
of bigoted sectarians and out-and-out materialists
is few but those few seem to be in authority and
able to persecute all those who may not be of their
way of thinking. The historical deficiency referred
to is by no means without a parallel. That super·
structure known as Christianity has, it is true,
many historical phases; of dogmas the most contradictory; of doctrines promulgated in one age, and
enforced with vice-regal authority, and severe pen-
alties for denial and disbelief, only to be denied and
repudiated as "damnable heresy" in another age.
In the meantime, the origin of these doctrines and
the personality of the *Man of Sorrows* around which
these traditions cluster receive no adequate sup·
port from authentic history.

Because there is no true history of the Christ to
be had, or because orthodox Churchanity has not

been able to produce such a history of whom they
make pretensions of following, but whom they have
never really *known*, must we conclude that it is all
a fable, that there was no Jesus of Nazareth, but
that it was put forth and kept alive by designing
men, to support their pretensions to authority?
Are historical facts and personal biography alone
entitled to credit? While everlasting principles,
Divine Beneficence, and the laying down of one's
life for another are of no account? Is that which
has inspired the hope and brightened the lives of
the down-trodden and despairing for ages a mere
fancy, a designing lie? Tear every shred of history
from the life of the *Christ*, today, and prove beyond
all controversy that he never existed, and Humanity, from its heart of hearts, would create him again
tomorrow and justify the creation by every intuition of the human soul and by every need of the
daily life of man. The historical contention might
be given up, ignored, and the whole character, genius and mission of *Jesus*, the *Christ*, be none the less
real, beneficent, and eternal, with all of its human
and dramatic episodes. Explain it as you will it
can never be explained away; the character remains;
and whether Historical or Ideal, it is *real* and *eternal*. The *Christ* was no myth.

This digression serves to illustrate a principle of
Interpretation. The Traditions and Symbols of
Mysticism and the Philosophy of Fire do not derive
their real value from historical data, but *from the
universal and eternal truths which they embody, and all
Orders and Fraternities are founded on these symbols of*

Mysticism and there is no Order, Masonry not excepted, but that is founded on the Philosophy of the Living Fire. Without Love no Order could exist. Love is the only bond that can bind men Eternally together. Were they historical episodes only, the world in its cyclic revolutions would long ago have swept by them and buried them in Eternal oblivion. They *are facts, imparted by Initiate to Initiate, from time out of memory, until the present time.* These great truths, obscured and lost in one age by misinterpretation or persecution, rise, Phoenix-like, rejuvenated in the next. I should not say lost, they are simply held in the secret Archives of the great Orders to be given out again when the time is ripe. They are *immortal truths*, knowing neither decay nor death. They are like Divine Images concealed in a block of stone, which many artists assail with mallet and chisel, square and compass, only, perchance, to release a distorted idol. Only the Master workman, the Adept, can so chip away the stone as to reveal in all its grandeur and beauty the *divine ideal*, and endow it with the breath of life. Such is the builder of character. Ceremonial Initiation will never make either a Master or an Adept. Any man or set of men can carry on Ceremonial Initiation. No Master can be made in this way. It takes a Master to take man in his crude or materialistic state, and make a Master out of him, and this can only be done by a process of growth and a rigid system of training.

No genuine Mystic, imbued with the spirit of liberality, and all Mystics are liberal, will treat any

religion with derision or contempt, or exclude from
fellowship any Brother who believes in the existence of God, the Universal Brotherhood of Man,
and the Immortality of the Soul.   This spirit is the
very foundation of Mysticism, and any departure
from it is un-Mystical and directly against the
spirit of Universal Brotherhood.   True Mysticism
has, for ages, held aloft the torch-light of Toleration,
Equity, and Fraternity. The bigoted sectarian, whoever he may be, divides the world into two classes;
those who, with zeal and blind faith, accept his dogmas and those who do not. The first he calls "brother," and the second class he regards as enemies
who must be persecuted.   Mysticism, no matter
what the school, while adopting no religion and no
form of doctrine or creed, as such, or as formulated by any one religion, recognizes certain basic
principles embodying the ethics taught in all religions.   *No religion, no matter how fanatical it may be,
could exist unless there was some truth in it.*   Every
Mystic formulates his own creed to suit himself and
according to the Light *within* his Soul, and may
institute such forms of worship, *for himself*, as may
seem to him desirable or beneficent.   As he grows
in wisdom he will give up the old forms for others
until at last, he will worship *at the very throne of the
Living Fire—Love—God.*

The distinction between the esoteric and exoteric
doctrines was always and from the very earliest
times preserved among the Initiates. It came from
Atlantis up to the time of Alexander and after that
they resorted for instructions, dogmas, and mys-

teries, to all the schools; to those of Egypt, and
Asia, as well as those of ancient Thrace, Sicily,
Etruria, and other countries.

The real source from whence the Ancient Wisdom came was Atlantis, thence to Egypt and old
India, the Mother of Civilizations and Religions,
and the esoteric or concealed wisdom.

The most profound secrets of Mysticism are not
revealed or taught in any Ceremonial Initiation.
They belong only to a few. These secrets must be
sought by the individual himself, and the Neophyte
is debarred from possessing them solely by his own
inattention to the hints everywhere given by the
Masters of the Fraternities. If he prefers to treat
the whole subject with contempt, and to deny that
any such *real* knowledge exists, it becomes evident
that he not only closes the door against the possibility of himself possessing such knowledge, but he
also becomes impervious of any evidence of its existence that might come to him at any time. He has
no one but himself to blame if he is left in darkness.
"Seek and ye shall find, Knock and it shall be
opened unto you."

"So long as the struggle for bare existence involves, as it does today, the greater part of the
energy, time, and opportunities of man, he will
never discover the *real* meaning of Life, or the purpose of human existence. Even this much may be
discerned from physical evolution alone; from the
study of the human brain, in which there is a continually increasing portion of gray substance set
free from the functions incident to the preserva-

tion of the physical structure, and evidently de-
signed to be appropriated to separate and Higher
use.   Mere intellectual activities alone, connected
with the physical plane, with the maintenance and
enjoyment of life will not explain the philosophy of
cerebral development.   It is largely for this reason
that the offices of the encephalon are so little
known today.

There are *latent powers* and almost infinite capa-
bilities in man, the meaning of which he has hardly
dreamed of possessing.   Nor will leisure and intellectual cultivation alone reveal these powers.   It is
only through a complete philosophy of the entire
nature of man and the capacities and destiny of the
human soul supplemented by the use of such knowledge, that man will eventually come into possession
of his birthright and begin the journey to perfection.   It is the work of the Masters to show man
the Path to such development and the Masters of
all ages and Fraternities *have* faithfully performed
this great work.

Two conditions at the present time stand squarely
in the way of such achievements : first, anarchy and
confusion, the result of selfishness in all social
relations.   This condition can be overcome in but
one way, viz: by the recognition of the unqualified
Brotherhood of Man; not as a theory, a religious
duty, or a mere matter of sentiment; but as a fact
in nature; a Universal and Divine Law; the penalty
for the violation of which is precisely the conditions
under which humanity now struggles and suffers.

The second condition, which has given rise to

"Confusion among the Workmen" in building the social temple and the individual habitation of man, is false ideals; inefficient methods of education; and almost total ignorance of the existence and the nature of the Soul. The result of this ignorance may be seen in the fact, that not one individual in a million who has both leisure and opportunity, makes any real advancement in the evolution of the higher powers or is even cognizant of the fact that he is a *living soul*.

These things ought not to be so, nor need they longer be, if earnest men and women would seek diligently, first for the cause of all our ills, and second, for a sufficient remedy. This remedy is to be found, first, in *knowledge*. Second, in service of the Truth.

If *real* knowledge of the nature of the Soul and the destiny of man had never existed, our present condition would be pitiable in the extreme; but when we demonstrate that this knowledge once existed, that it still exists, and that it always existed, even though only in the Secret Archives of the Orders, that it was first degraded by selfishness and then lost by design, and that for centuries designing Priests, many of whom would have disgraced a scaffold, but who have been canonized as saints, have done their utmost to deprive humanity of this knowledge, what shall humanity say? Shall he preach Universal Brotherhood and Toleration, and yet seek revenge on the priesthood? A thousand times, no! but rather leave priest and proletariat to settle their own affairs and go their own way, and go to work *ourselves* to recover the *lost knowledge*, and when recovered devote it absolutely to Humanity. Knowing these things as we do, can we condemn the Arch Fraternities who have ever been the guardians of this Secret Knowledge? Should we not rather be thankful to them for keeping it in its virgin purity? In all our *popular* present religious instructions, from childhood, and through all the ministrations of religion in after life, we are taught to look very sharp after the salvation of our souls; and this in the face of the statement that a very large proportion of the human race will eventually be utterly lost, or damned, for all eternity! Science (?) completes the picture by trying to demonstrate that the struggle for existence is a necessary condition for all improvements; and that only the sharpest tooth and longest claw can survive. The ideal thus held aloft by both religion and science, of the present time, is pure *selfishness*. Self-preservation is regarded as the "*First Law of Life.*" The result is *Materialism* in the strictest and broadest sense, and this has paralyzed where it has not utterly destroyed, all *higher* ideals. What are the results? In Science it leads to the horrible crime of Vivisection, with its Serum Therapy and demand for human beings for experiment, and in Religion we have a pure materialism. Man for himself, while the Law teaches us to *give* life and thereby *win* it.\

Is it not reasonable to suppose that if humanity were possessed of *real* knowledge it might govern its actions, and so shape their lives as to avoid the pitfalls of ignorance, and set its feet on the line of the Higher Evolution? Religion, true religion, that which comes from the heart, offers Faith, and in Faith all things are possible. Such religion is pure Mysticism.

There is but one source of *real* knowledge, viz; Mysticism and Philosophy. The twain are one, and these have taken their rise directly, from the Ancient Mysteries. The Universal Brotherhood of Man must be, and is, the only basis of true Ethics, and the Great Republic is the Ideal State. If these concepts were accepted and acted upon, there would result, time, opportunity, and the power to apprehend the deeper and higher problems of the origin, nature, and destiny of man. "Man is not man as yet, and will not be until he has found his Soul." What he may be or what he might do, under favorable conditions, is very seldom dreamed of by humanity and is only shown to us by the lives of the few Masters.

There is a widespread and increasing conviction that true Education would prove a panacea for all our evils; and that if we could begin with the training of children, we could eventually reform society, even the children of vicious parentage might be reformed.

This is true but it will not be enough to follow the lines of education as at present used. We must have a real, an Higher education, the education of the Soul. The bringing out of the Highest in man. Only by teaching the child the truth, not as supposed to be by material or theological educators, but as the Soul teaches man what is right. Selfishness or material gain, is the key-note of the present day education and it is for this reason that it has failed so miserably. Nothing so shrouds the Higher Self (the Soul) in man as selfishness, and this is the reason why so few persons are possessed of the direct perception. What is true, is True, and what is false, is False.

It is this Higher knowledge toward which all useful and rational acquirement tends; and why should our efforts cease short of the very Highest? All education that does not tend in this direction, with the final goal consistently and continually in view, is false, and is necessarily a failure. This Higher knowledge or Philosophy, is a knowledge of the Soul; of its origin, nature, powers, and the laws that govern its evolution; and this is precisely the knowledge which modern science fails to afford, but which Ancient Science taught in the Mysteries of Antiquity which was nothing short of the Philosophy of the Living Fire (Soul). All preliminary study and training led up to this—"The real measure of a man." Just as all life is an evolution, so is all *real* knowledge or Philosophy an *Initiation*; and it proceeds in a Natural order, and advances by specific "degrees." These "degrees" are now materialized in the Modern Masonic Fraternity, an Order that has all the material and hidden wisdom of the Mysteries of Antiquity, but which has lost the key, excepting in a few instances. In the *true* Initiation, the candidate must always be worthy and well qualified, duly and truly prepared. That is, he must perceive that such knowledge exists; must *desire* to possess it, and must be willing to make whatever personal sacrifice is necessary for its acquirement. He must have passed beyond the stage of blind belief or superstition, the bondage of fear, the age of fable, and the dominion of appetite and sense. This is the meaning of being "duly and truly prepared." He must have proved his fitness in these directions, no less than the absence in him of that subtler form of intellectual selfishness which comes from the possession of knowledge, and the desire for dominion through it over others less highly endowed, for selfish purposes of his own. His motive, therefore, alone, can determine that he is "worthy and well qualified."

It is true on every plane of life, that in the process by which knowledge is acquired—always by experience—man becomes the thing which he knows. That is, knowing is a progressive *becoming*. There results, therefore, a continuous transformation of the motives, ideals, and perceptions of the individual, whenever in his daily experience in life he is placed on the lines of least resistance or the Natural Order of Evolution. This is the really Scientific and Philosophical meaning of all *true* Initiation.

There is, at present, so much of the commonplace that passes as knowledge, and which is accepted as such by worthy, though unthinking students, and this is so utterly void of comprehension, that unless one is familiar with this line of thought he will not really see the truth and bearing of the statement, that man always *becomes* that which he really knows. Here lies the reason why the mere inculcation of moral precepts so often fails entirely in transforming character; and why there is so much lip-service. When men once understand this, then they will understand the Mystery of Alchemy, the Transformation or Transmutation of baser metals into the pure and shining gold. For once they understand, once the Conscience has become awakened and they have learned to know, then they will have *become*, for in the process of truly learning to *know*, they will have *become*.

Conscience is the struggle of the understanding in assimilating experience; it is the effort of the individual to adjust precept with practice, or in other words, Conscience is that *living, active* process, resulting in the growth of the Soul, and in the increase of man's power to apprehend the truth. Thus, while he is learning he is actually growing or Transmuting, and the process will be finished ere he knows it.

In the Ancient Mysteries, Life presented itself to the candidate or Neophyte, as a problem to be solved, and not as certain propositions to be memorized and as easily forgotten. The solution of this problem constituted all genuine Initiation, and at every step or "degree" the problem expanded. For this reason was "Man, *know thyself*" written above the door of every temple of Initiation. As the vision of the Neophyte enlarged in relation to the problems and meaning of life, his powers of apprehension and assimilation also increased pro-

portionately. This was also an evolution. The
lower degrees of such Initiation concerned the
ordinary affairs of life, viz: a knowledge of the laws
and processes of external nature; the Neophyte's
relation to these through his physical body, and his
relations, on the physical plane, through his animal
senses and social instincts, to his fellow men.
These things being learned, not memorized, the
Neophyte passed on to the next degree. He here
learned the nature of his Soul: the process of its
evolution, and began to unfold those finer instincts
that have been so often referred to in works dealing
with Initiation. If he was found capable of understanding these, and kept his vow in the preceding
degrees, he presently discovered the evolution
within him of senses and faculties pertaining to the
"soul-plane." His progress would be instantly
arrested, and his teachers would refuse all further
instructions, if he was found negligent of the ordinary duties of life; those to his family, his neigh-
bors, or his country. All these must have been
fully discharged before he could stand upon the
threshold of the Greater Mysteries; for in these he
came to be an unselfish servant to Humanity as a
whole; and no longer the right to bestow the gifts
of knowledge or power that he possessed, upon his
own kinsmen, or friends, in preference to strangers.
In the higher degrees, he might be precluded from
using these powers even to preserve his own life.
Both the Master and his powers belongs to Humanity. If the reader will but consider how the
Jews called upon the Christ to "save himself and

come down from the cross," if he were the Christ,
it may be seen that this doctrine of Supreme Selfishness ought, long ago, to have been apprehended
by the Christian world; for while it is a Divine
Attribute, the Synonym of the Christ, it is latent
in all humanity, and must be evolved as herein
given.

That which makes such an evolution seem to
modern readers impossible, is, that it cannot be
conceived as being accomplished in a single life, nor
can it be. It is the result of persistent effort guided
by High Ideals through many lives. Those who
deny Pre-existence may logically deny all such evolution. There must, however, come a time when
the consummation is reached in one life; and this
is the logical meaning of the saying of the Christ
—*It is finished.*

At this day, even many of those who have not the
honor to belong to any of the Higher Secret Fraternities, know that there was both an exoteric and
an esoteric doctrine with the early Christians; that
the esoteric doctrines were communicated orally in
the Mysteries of Initiation; and that these Mysteries conformed to and were originally derived
from those of the *so-called* Pagan world. The Mysteries of Christ received a new interpretation after
the first Nicene Council, and as the Church sought
dominion, it lost the Great Secret, and since then
has denied that it ever existed, and has done all in its
power to obliterate all its records and monuments.

That this is absolutely true, we can prove, not
alone by the Secret Manuscripts which we, of these

Orders hold, but by history. Tertullian, who died about A- D. 216, says in his *apology:* "None are admitted to the religious Mysteries without an oath of Secrecy. We appeal to your Thracian and Eleusinian Mysteries; and we are specially bound to this caution, because if we prove faithless, we should not only provoke Heaven, but draw upon our heads the utmost rigor of human displeasure."

Archelaus, Bishop of Cascara in Mesopotamia, the year 278, said: "These mysteries the church now communicates to him who has passed through the introductory degree. These are not explained to the Gentiles at all; nor are they taught in the hearing of the Catechumens, but much that is spoken is in disguised terms, that the Faithful, who possess the knowledge, may be still more informed, and those who are not acquainted with it may suffer no disadvantage."

The Council of Nice had not taken these Secret Fraternities into consideration, nor did they know much of these Fraternities. They had knowledge of such Orders but were under the impression that they were only for the purpose of Pagan Initiatlons. They did not know that these Orders had records that would be handed down from Initiate to Initiate for all times to come, and that the Keys to these Sacred Mysteries could never be lost to these Fraternities. Had they known of this, they might have made different changes. Again, we find that St. Basil, the great Bishop of Caesarea, says:

"We receive the dogmas transmitted to us by writing, and those which have descended to us from the Apostles, and beneath the Mystery of Oral tradition; for several things have been handed to us without writing, lest the vulgar, too familiar with our dogmas, should lose a due respect for them. This is what the *Uninitiated* are not permitted to contemplate; and how should it ever be proper to write and circulate among the people an account of them."

The men who composed the Council of Nice knew that there were those, Priests, who claimed to know these Secret Mysteries but they were called more mad than anything else, exactly as our Churchmen think of the greater Mystics of our day.

The Universal Science and the Sublime Philosophy, once taught by the Atlantians, later in the Greater Mysteries of Egypt, India, Chaldea, Asia and Persia, and among many other nations of antiquity, is neither known to Modern Christianity, Masonry or any of the other Exoteric Orders. They may be Initiators of Ceremonial degrees but the Mystic Fraternities alone have preserved the Key to these Initiations and have kept the teachings in their purity.

The Ancient Mysteries, or Mysteries of Antiquity were first taught in the Temples of Atlantis and spread from thence as has already been stated. These Mysteries were taught, under many different names, up to the time of the Initiation of Christ into the Essenian Order or Fraternity. After this date they naturally took the name of Christian Mysteries. For the very reason that Christ was one of their Arch-Initiates.

In the year 525, B. C.; Cambyces, called "the mad," led an army into Egypt, overran the country, destroyed its cities, palaces and temples, scattered its Priest-Initiates (all Priests of the temples were not only Initiates into these Mysteries, but were Masters since they were the appointed teachers of the Neophytes), and reduced the country to a Persian province. Many of its priests took refuge in Greece, and conveyed thither the Egyptian Mysteries (these Mysteries should really have been called the Atlantian Mysteries), which Pythagoras had journeyed to Egypt to obtain half a century earlier. In the time of Plato, a century later, the Mysteries were in a flourishing condition, and in them he learned his sublime Philosophy. At the beginning of the Christian era, the mysteries were known only to the Initiates and Priests and the masses were in ignorance as to their existence. There remained, at the time, the Essenian Order and also the Gnostics, the latter being an Inner Circle of the Essenes. The Therapeutiae of Alexandria was simply another name for a Circle of the Essenian Fraternity. Today the Order then known as the Essenes is known as the Fraternity of the Rosy Cross. There has never been any interruption of the Secret Order. It has changed its name many times since it was founded on the Atlantis, but its teachings are the same. Thus, from these Orders the Christian Mysteries were derived and are preserved in the Secret Archives of all true Occult Orders, known only to the Initiates of the Higher Degrees. The Neoplatonists, headed by

Ammonius Saccus, undertook to preserve the primitive relation, and the utterances of the Christian Bishops to which reference has been made, show how the Secret Doctrine was adopted from the earlier mysteries by the primitive Christians during the first three centuries of our era. After the first Council of Nice, A. D., 325, which was presided over by none other than Exoteric Christians looking for power and authority, little more was heard of the earlier doctrines, and with the burning of the Great Library of Alexandria, Catholic supremacy and the dark ages obliterated the primitive wisdom of Western Europe, so far as the masses were concerned, as it was overrun by hordes of Barbarians from the north. The principal seats of learning were the convents. Coming now to the dawn of the 16th century, and the greatest Protestant and Rosicrucian Reformation, we find Johann Trithemius. Abbott of St. Jacob, at Wurtzburg, celebrated as one of the greatest Alchemists and Adepts; and Cornelius Agrippus and Paracelsus were his pupils. We must not forget Christian Rosencreutz, the Refounder of the Rosicrucian Fraternity, and the powerful influence his works had on the reformation of those times. John Reuchlin, a famous Kabalist, of that time, and counted as one of the most learned men of his day, in Europe, was the friend and preceptor of Luther, and Luther's first public utterances were a course of lectures on the Philosophy of Aristotle. What effect the Rosicrucian Reformation had on Luther is not positively known. However we do know that Luther used as his private seal the Rose and the Cross. A strong effort was made to revive the Ancient Wisdom among those outside of the Inner Circle of the Secret Fraternities, but the age was too gross and superstitious, and the reformation resulted in centuries of blind belief, and the suppression of the Secret Doctrine. However, the Universal Reformation had accomplished one of its purposes, it had drawn to itself those who were *truly* ready to be received by the Mighty Secret Fraternity. Our records show us that this is an absolute fact.

Students should always bear In mind the fact that in *all* the truly Secret Fraternities, there has always been, and will ever be, an Exoteric portion given out to the world, to the *Unitiated*, and an Esoteric portion *reserved* for the *Initiate*, and revealed by *degrees*, according as the Neophyte demonstrates his fitness to receive, conceal, and rightly use the knowledge so imparted. Few professed Christians are, perhaps, aware that such was the case with Christianity from its earliest times up to the present and that such must continue to be the case for all times to come, until men reach perfection.

All *true* Occult Fraternities recognize the whole world as but one Republic, of which each Nation is a family, and every individual a child, not in any wise derogating from the differing duties which the diversity of states requires, tends to create a new people, which, composed of many nations and tongues, shall be bound together by the bonds of a *true* Science, the belief of the Fatherhood of an All-wise Being and the Universal Brotherhood of Man.

Therefore, the real object of these Orders, be they Mystic Masonry or any other Mystic or Occult Fraternities, may be summed up in the following: To efface from among men the prejudices of caste, the conventional distinctions of color, origin, opinion, nationality; to annihilate fanaticism and superstition, extirpate national discord and with it extinguish the firebrand of war; in a word—to arrive, by free and pacific progress, at one formula or model of eternal and universal right, according to which each individual human being shall be free to develop every faculty with which he may be endowed, and to concur heartily and with all the fullness of his strength, in the bestowment of happiness upon all, and thus to make of the whole human race one family of brothers, united by Love, Wisdom and Science.

In order to do this, a true and beautiful Philosophy must be taught.   True Science and Religion must be wedded together and the Key to both Science and Religion or Philosophy must be God—Love.   Such a Philosophy are we ever ready to teach and only by so doing can a Universal Brotherhood of Man be founded.

The essential form or *idea* of *all* things; the potency or force; and the matter as we now discern it, must have existed in primordial space.   Therefore, these two always exist, viz: the *inner* potency, and the outer act; the concealed Idea, and the outer form; the *inner* meaning and the outer event.   Each in turn a symbol of the other.   Hence the saying on the Smaragdine Table of Hermes, *as above, so below.* All outward things are therefore symbols, or embodiments of pre-existing Ideas, and out of this subjective Ideal realm all visible things have *emanated.* This doctrine of emanations is the key to the Philosophy of Plato, and that of the Gnostic and Essene sects from which the early Christians derived their *Mysteries.*

There is a Grand Science known as Magic, and every Real Master of any Order must be a Magician. Feared by the ignorant, and ridiculed by the supposedly "learned," the Divine Science and its Masters have, nevertheless, existed in all ages, and exist today as surely as the Orders or Fraternities exist in which they are the Masters. Occultism in its deeper meaning and recondite mysteries constitutes and possesses this Science, and all genuine Initiation consists in an unfolding of the natural powers of the Neophyte, so that he shall become the very thing he desires to possess. In seeking Magic, he finally becomes the Magi. All genuine Initiation is like evolution and regeneration from within. Devoid of this Inner meaning and power, all Rituals and Ceremonial Initiations are but foolish jargon and without meaning to the Initiated. That the Christ-life and power that made Jesus to be called Christos, Master, whereby he healed the sick cast out devils, and foretold future events, is the same Life revealed by Initiation in the Greater Mysteries of Antiquity, is perfectly plain. The disrepute into which the Divine Science has fallen has arisen from its abuse and degradation.

There are dangers inseparable from Symbolism and Mysticism, which afford an impressive lesson in regard to similar risks attendant on the use of

secret forces. The Imagination called in to assist
the reason usurps its place, or leaves its ally helplessly entangled in its web. Names which stand for
things are confounded with them; the means are
mistaken for the ends; the instrument of interpretation for the object; and thus symbols come to
usurp an independent character as truths and persons. Though perhaps a necessary path, they are
a dangerous one, by which to approach the Deity;
in which many, says Plutarch, mistaking the sign
for the thing signified, fell into a ridiculous superstition, while others, in avoiding one extreme,
plunge into the no less hideous gulf of irreligion
and impiety.

It is through the Mysteries, Cicero says, that we
have learned the first principles of Life, wherefore
the term "Initiation" is used with good reason.

To employ Nature's Universal Symbolism instead
of the technicalities of language, rewards the hum-
blest inquirer and discloses its secrets to everyone
in proportion to his preparatory training to comprehend them. If their Philosophical meaning was
above the comprehension of some, their moral and
political meanings are within the reach of all.

In every age there have been dabblers in magic
as there are at the present time; sorcerers and nec-
romancers, who, possessing some of the secrets,
and imbued with none of its beneficence, have used
this knowledge and power for purely personal and
selfish ends. Hypnotism and Phenomenal Spiritualism are sufficient illustrations of the power
referred to, and the abuse to which it may be put.

Magic, *per se*, is always an absolute Science, and
up to a certain point it may be cultivated without
regard to its use, or the well-being of man; although
any abuse of it will prove fatal to the magician
sooner or later and the black Magician will eventually destroy himself.

The popular idea is that education consists largely
in the cultivation of the intellectual powers. An
average standard of morals is always recommended
by educators, and its outer form is illustrated by
religious ceremonies. But intellectual cultivation
alone, no matter to what extent it may be carried—
and the further it goes on in this one-sided way the
worse for all concerned—is in no sense an evolution, as such one-sided education is the cause of our
present day bigotism and extreme narrow-minded-
ness. Perfect intellectual development, without
spiritual discernment and moral obligation, is the
sign-manual of *Satan:* Intelligence, without goodness, lies athwart the Divine Plan in the evolution
of Cosmos. Intellect and Altruism by no means
necessarily go hand in hand. One may have a very
clear intellect, have quick perceptions, and be a
good reasoner, and yet a perfect scoundrel. On the
other hand, the one may be very dull intellectually,
and yet be kind, brotherly and sympathetic to the last
degree. A world made up of the former would be a
bad place to live in; if of the latter, a thousand times
to be preferred. Magic contemplates that all-around
development which, liberating the intellect from
the dominion of the senses and illuminating the
Spiritual Perceptions, places the individual on the

THE PHILOSOPHY OF FIRE   52

lines of least resistance with the Inflexible Laws of
Nature, and he becomes Nature's co-worker or
hand-maid.   To all such, Nature makes obeisance,
and delegates her powers, and they become Masters.   The real Master conceals his power and uses
it only for the good of others.   He works "without
the hope of fee or reward," knowing that God is just.

Knowing that "Knowledge is Power," designing
and evil men desire to possess both knowledge and
power for entirely selfish purposes.   It may be
readily understood that the more knowledge and
power a purely selfish man possesses, the more
inimical to humanity he becomes.   He can do less
harm if kept in ignorance.   This is especially the
case with those Deeper Sciences which deal with
Mind, and influence the thoughts and actions of
others.   *Modern Science, purely materialistic in its
aims and conclusions, has always ridiculed the idea embodied in Magic, for materialism can never recognize
the Spiritual.*

The traditional Lost Word of the Master is a key
to all the science of Magic, but it must be remem-
bered that the Lost Word is *not* a Word, but refers
to Spiritual Awakening; Spiritual Development;
the finding of the *Christ within the heart of man.*   The
knowledge of the Master is not empirical.   It does
not consist of a few isolated formulas by which certain startling or unusual effects can be produced.
Formulas have nothing to do with this knowledge.
*He has found and knows his own soul, he has purified
the heart so that it throbs with Love for Humanity and
through the re-awakening of Instinct and Intuition, he*

holds the key to the Universe and therefore uses Nature's Laws whereby to do his work. He does not work contrary to Natural Laws, but in harmony with them. The Magician's art is therefore based on a Science far deeper and more exact than modern physical science has yet dreamed of, and back of this science lies a Philosophy as boundless as the Universe, as inexhaustible as Time, and as beneficent as the "Father in Heaven."

Such men, such Masters—of themselves, have always existed, and no book or record worth preserving or in any way necessary for the good of man is ever lost. In the secret Crypts, alike inaccessible to the hands of Uninitiated man, and the corrosion of time and decay, these Records are well preserved and can only be made use of by those who are truly prepared and are fit to make use of their teachings.

All human progress runs in cycles. Modern materialistic science has had its brief day and must gradually give way. True philosophy has already undermined its foundations. The new age will show a genuine revival of Philosophy and true Science.

The immortal principles enunciated by Plato, clothed in modern garb of thought, less involved and dialectical, will again command the attention of the thinking world. Every one is aware that the source of Plato's knowledge was the Mysteries; he was an Initiate, and on almost every page reveals the obligation he is under not to betray to the common people the secrets taught only to Initiates under the pledge of secrecy.

There is in Nature one most potent force, by
means of which, a single man, who could possess
himself of it, and should know how to direct it,
could revolutionize and change the whole face of the
world. This force was known to the Ancients and
the secret is still held by the true Mystic Fraternities of this day. It is a Universal agent, whose
supreme law is equilibrium; and whereby, if science can but learn how to control it, it will be possible to change the order of the Seasons; to produce
in night the phenomena of day; to send a thought
in an instant around the world; to heal or slay at a
distance; to give our words universal success, and
make them reverberate everywhere.

There is a Life-Principle of the world, a universal
agent, wherein are two natures and a double current of love and wrath. This ambient fluid pervades
everything. It is a ray detached from the glory of
the Sun, and fixed by the weight of the atmosphere
and the central attraction. It is the body of the
Holy Spirit, the Universal Agent, the Serpent
devouring his own tail.

With this electro-magnetic ether, this vital and
luminous caloric, the Ancients and the Alchemists
were familiar. Of this agent, that phase of modern
ignorance termed physical science, talks incoher-
ently, knowing nothing of it save its effects; and theology might apply to it all its pretended definitions
of spirit.

Quiescent, it is appreciable by no human sense;
disturbed, or in movement, none can explain its
mode of action except a real Master, and to term it

a "fluid" and speak of its "currents," is but to veil a profound ignorance under a cloud of words.

The Bible, with all the allegories it contains, ex‹ presses, in a veiled and incomplete manner only, the religious science of the Hebrews. The doctrines of Moses and the prophets, identical at bottom with that of the ancient Egyptians, also had its outer meaning and its veils. The Hebrew books were written only to recall to memory the traditions; and they were written in Symbols unintelligible to the Profane. The Pentateuch and the prophetic poems were merely elementary books of doctrines, morals or liturgy; and the *true* secret and traditional phil‹ osophy was only written afterwards, under a veil still less transparent. This was a second Bible born, unknown to, or rather uncomprehended by, the Christians of later times, "a collection, they say, of monstrous absurdities; a monument, the Adept says, wherein is everything that the genius of Phil‹ osophy and that of religion have ever formed or im‹ agined of the Sublime; a treasure surrounded by thorns; a diamond concealed in a rough dark stone."

The Kabalah then, alone consecrates the alliance of the Universal Reason and Divine Word; it estab‹ lishes, by the counterpoise of two forces apparently opposite, the eternal balance of being; it alone rec‹ onciles Reason with Faith, and Power with Liberty, Science with Mystery; it has the keys of the Pres‹ ent, the Past, and the Future.

One is filled with admiration on penetrating into the Sanctuary of the Kabalah, at seeing a doctrine so logical, so simple and at the same time so absolute. The necessary union of ideas and signs, the consecration of the most fundamental realities by the primitive characters; the Trinity of Words, Letters and Numbers; a Philosophy simple as the alphabet, profound and infinite as the World; Theorems more complete and luminous than those of Pythagoras; a theology summed up by counting on one's fingers; an Infinite which can be held in the hollow of an infant's hand, ten ciphers and twenty-two letters, a triangle, a square and a circle—these are all the elements of the Kabalah. These are the elementary principles of the written Word, reflection of that spoken Word that created the world.

Life may be represented by a Triangle, at the apex of which is God. Of this triangle the two sides are formed by two streams, the one flowing outwards, the other upwards. The base may be taken to represent the material plane. Thus, from God proceed the Gods. From the Gods proceed all the Hierarchy of heaven, with the various orders from the highest to the lowest. Here again we have the Doctrine of Hermes.

The Kabalah of the ancient Hebrews, which Moses derived by Initiation into the Mysteries of Egypt and Persia, was identical among the Hebrews, the Egyptians, Hindus and other nations of antiquity, was known as the *Secret Doctrine.*

Initiation is knowledge unfolded by degrees in an orderly, systematic way, step by step, as the capacity to apprehend opens in the Neophyte. The result is not a possession, but a growth, an evolution. Knowledge is not a mere sum in addition; something added to some-

thing that already exists; but rather such a progressive change of transformation of the original structure as to make of it at every step a New Being. Real Knowledge, or the growth of Wisdom in Man, is an Eternal Becoming; a progressive transformation into the likeness of the Supreme Goodness and Supreme Power.

The Sacred Books of all religions, including those of the Jews and the Christians, were and are no more than parables and allegories of the *real* Secret Doctrines, transcribed for the ignorant and superstitious masses. All commentaries written on these Sacred Books, whether on those of Moses, the Psalms and the Prophets of Judaism, the Gospels of the Gnostics and Christians, or those written on the Sacred Books of the East—the Vedas, Puranas, and Upanishads—all either make confusion more confounded when written by one ignorant of the Secret Doctrine, or, when written by Initiates, but bring the changes on, or further elaborate the parables and allegories.

It is easily demonstrable that the Secret Doctrine came originally from Atlantis, and is the Primitive Wisdom Religion. Its earlier records are now found in Asia, Egypt, and India and from thence carried through other countries.

Underlying this Secret Doctrine is a profound philosophy of the creation or evolution of worlds and of man. The present humanity in many quarters of the globe, has evolved on the intellectual plane so far that there now exist a very large number of persons capable of apprehending this old philosophy, and, at the same time, capable of understanding the responsibility incurred in misusing or misinterpreting it. A large number of persons have reached, on the intellectual plane, the state of manhood; and are capable of partaking of the "fruit of the tree of knowledge of Good and Evil." There is, therefore, no reason why this old philosophy should be longer concealed. On the other hand, there are reasons why it should be known. Empirical knowledge has advanced in certain directions into the realm of Psychism, and the arts anciently designated by the term *Magic*, and it is imperative that the dangers that attend these pursuits should be pointed out and demonstrated, in order that they may be avoided by the beneficent, and that the ignorant or innocent may be afforded protection. How far these modern inroads into Occultism or ancient Magic extended very few persons seem to realize. It is therefore high time that the Philosophy of the East should illumine the science of the West, and thus give the death blow to that intellectual diabolism, and spiritual nihilism, known as Materialism, and this only the Secret Doctrine can accomplish. Grave responsibility, however, is incurred by such a revelation. Those who, like the professional Hypnotist and the Vivisectionists, have sinned, perhaps ignorantly, and thus have been unconsciously "Black Magicians," will eventually find no avenue of escape.

As I am preparing the above, I receive a clipping entitled "The Mystic Side of the Bacillus Theory," by that Master of both Medicine and the Secret Doctrine, Dr J. R. Phelps. Since Serum Therapy and Vivisection go hand in hand, I think it well to reproduce the article as it will show that we are reaching a state where true knowledge is demanded.

"The man who has the temerity to question, or even discuss in a questioning way, the generally accepted basic principles that underlie his profession, is apt to find himself set down a heretic, and invites the sneers and inuendoes, if not crucifixion, of those who accept the deductions of scientists, and deny the right of speech to anyone who dares to be wise above what is written. Not that it follows, by any means, that the heretic is necessarily right any more than it follows that the human scientist is always right. For science has a large rubbish-heap in its back yard, on which may be found many a discarded plank that once formed part of its infallible platform.

"A scientist once told me that a drop of nitric acid applied to a piece of freshly broken granite revealed, under the microscope, numerous living things similar to animalculae found in stagnant water. 'This,' he asserted, 'proves that the solid rock is full of life!' I fail to see that it proves any such thing. It simply shows that the action of the acid produced a form of motion there, and wherever there is motion there is a magnetic current, and forms having life spring into existence—not that they were any more in the rock than in the acid, or that necessarily they were in either.

"After all, is there not as much mystery about the manifestation of life in matter as there is about thought action? Things become perceptible to us when they come within the range of the senses, but have they no form of existence before they come into this plane? Or do things spring from nothing?

"It has become the fashion, when there is a diseased bodily condition, to go on a hunt for the bacillus that is one of the manifestations of that condition. I have nothing to say against this proceeding, but it is a mistake to allow this research to close up every other avenue of investigation, and assume, offhand, that the bacillus is the *creator* of the disease, rather than its *creation*. And there are many of our profession who are thinking along this same line.

" If we read of the cures effected by the Divine Master (call him 'The Nazarene,' if you please, I don't care for names), we find His cures almost invariably prefixed by the words, 'Thy sins be forgiven thee;' and this declaration was always an offense to the pharasaical beholder. They could recognize the fact that a paralytic had been strangely healed, a leper cleansed, when the paralyzed man walked off with his bed on his back, or the hue of health came back to the pallid, ulcerated countenance; but the *word of power* that reached beyond their vision, and changed the mental condition that produced the disease, was too much for their comprehension.

"Let me quote from a writer on Mystical subjects: 'Disease does not enter in any manner from without. That which is external, simply awakens that which is already within us. Disease is not a thing—it is simply a depolarization. That sights

and sounds lure the imagination into activity, I
claim, and in this faculty of the mind depolarization of the spirit's action takes place, which causes
a sudden condensation of spirit in some parts of
the system, to the damage of other parts left desti-
tute.   Thus the system is all thrown out of harmony, because the normal action of spirit is
disturbed.

"Now, belief being the fundamental principle of
power, and man being more physical than mental,
his belief is more readily aroused and sustained by
physical substances than by ideas; hence, the Magi
used charms, amulets and talismans to inspire the
belief of the ignorant and material.

"Furthermore, who can doubt for a moment that
drugs, metals, vegetable substances, etc., have a
peculiar affinity for, or are antipathetic to, that
department of the spiritual nature which we call
the Imagination?

All action is dual—direct and reflex.   If material
substances act and create mental conditions—which
I do not deny—then mental conditions act on and
create material things.   The impure, diseased imagination, finding in the physical organism soil
suitable for the purpose, impregnates it and gener-
erates bacilli.   To *deny* this hypothesis does not *dis-
prove* it.   The bacteriologist, with his microscope,
discovers bacilli, and assumes that they are self-
created or produced by material, chemical action
of the physical atoms.   This may answer as explanation of maggots in rotten cheese, but the house
of an immortal thing, which we call soul or spirit,

is something different.   There is no motion of mus-
cles, tendon or ligament that is not started first by
mental action and will, *through*, (not *by*) the
brain.   And there is not a bacillus or microbe
infesting the blood or tissues, that did not have a
definite, positive existence before it became manifest to the microscope; and if we understand the
workings of mind as well as we do the anatomy of
the body (and there are some facts regarding this,
even, that we are ignorant of), we might get more
control over disease than we now seem to possess.
And even with this influence over the mind, what
do we do when an epidemic of cholera breaks out?
We set people to cleaning out their back yards, dis-
posing of rubbish, and, more important still, try to
teach them to keep themselves clean, and this occupation tends to produce a (temporary, at least),
condition of mental cleanliness.   Washing the *outside* of cup and platter is something in the way of
removing filth, and it is an accomplishment of some
moment to teach some men the religion of a clean
shirt.   Mental uncleanliness is apt to generate
bodily uncleanliness, and then the bacillus is a logical sequence.

"There is much attention being directed of late
to prophylactic treatment.   Would it not be as well
to extend this system a little further, and see if it
is not possible to pass over the border a little way
—cross the fence which science has erected between the realm of matter and the realm of the imponderable, and see if, after all, there may not be
something to be accomplished in the way of regu-

lation of disease before the enemy effects his invasion of the land? I believe we can meet with some measure of success, if we divest ourselves of some of our preconceived notions, and cease to take counsel of our denials, our limitations, our fears. It may be that there is something to be learned by looking at the bacillus theory from the Mystic side. For, let the materialist doubt, and scout, and deny, as he will, there *is* that side of the question, and it is every day forcing itself more and more into recognition. 'There are more things in heaven and earth than are dreamed of in our philosophy,' *and there always will be.*"

This then, is Science and Religion wedded. Had we more such teachers we would soon have a *true* Science but we must wait a little while longer. There can be no lines drawn as to where material science ends and Spiritual science begins. Therefore, the two should be as one.

They know little of the forces at work, or the principles involved, who imagine that there is sufficient force in dissolving creeds, or in the dying throes of materialism, to greatly retard the progress of these truths by sneers or ridicule, or to prevent their triumph by any opposition that can bring to bear against them.

The Secret Doctrine was the universally diffused religion of the ancient prehistoric world. Proof of its diffusion, authentic records of its history, a complete chain of documents, showing its character and presence in every land, together with the teachings of all its great Adepts or Masters, exist

to this day in the secret crypts of libraries belonging to the Occult Fraternities.

The days of Constantine were the last turning
point in history.   The period of the Supreme struggle that ended in the Western world throttling the
old religions in favor of the new ones, built on their
bodies.   From thence the vista into the far distant
Past, beyond the "Deluge" and the "Garden of
Eden," began to be forcibly and relentlessly closed
by every fair and unfair means against the indis-
creet gaze of posterity.   Every issue was blocked
up, every record that hands could be laid upon,
destroyed.

This same Constantine who, with his soldiers,
environed the Bishops at the first Council of Nice,
A. D., 325, and dictated terms to their delibera-
tions, applied for Initiation into the Mysteries, and
was told by the officiating priest that no purgation
could free him from the crime of putting his wife
to death, or from his many perjuries and murders.
Every careful and unbiased student of history
knows why the Secret Doctrine has been heard of
so little since the days of Constantine.   An exoteric
religion, and belief in a personal God blotted it out
of self-protection; and yet, the very Pentateuch
conceals it, and for many a student of the Kabalah,
of the coming century, the seals will be broken.

There are three fundamental propositions that
underlie the Secret Doctrine. (1.) "An omnipresent, Eternal, Boundless, and Immutable Principle on which all speculation is impossible, since
it transcends the power of human conception, and

could only be dwarfed by any human expression or similitude. It is beyond the range and reach of human thought—in the words of Mandykya, "unthinkable and upspeakable." This Infinite and Eternal Cause—dimly formulated in the "Unconscious" and "Unknowable" of current European Philosophy—is the rootless root of "all that was, is, or ever shall be." In Sanskrit it is "Sat." This "Beness" is symbolized in the Secret Doctrine under two aspects.

On the one hand, Absolute abstract Space, representing bare subjectivity, the one thing which no human mind can either exclude from any conception or conceive of by itself.

On the other hand, Absolute abstract Motion representing "Unconditioned Consciousness." Spirit (or Consciousness) and Matter are, however, to be regarded, not as independent realities, but as the two facets or aspects of the Absolute, which constitutes the basis of conditional Being whether subjective or objective. "Considering this metaphysical triad" (the one reality, Spirit and Matter) "as the root from which proceeds all manifestation, the 'Great Breath' assumes the character of precosmic Ideation."

(2) The second of the three postulates of the Secret Doctrine is: "The Eternity of the Universe in toto as a boundless plane: periodically 'the playground of numberless Universes incessantly manifesting and disappearing,' called 'the manifesting stars' and the 'sparks of Eternity.' 'The Eternity of the Pilgrim' (the Monad or Self in man) is like a

5

wink of the Eye of Self-Existence. 'The appearance and disappearance of worlds is like a regular tidal ebb of flux and reflux.' "

(3) "The fundamental identity of all Souls with the Universal Over-Soul, the latter being itself an aspect of the Unknown Root; and the obligatory pilgrimage for every Soul—a spark of the former—through the Cycle of Incarnation in accordance with Cyclic and Karmic law, during the whole term." "The pivotal doctrine of the Eastern Philosophy admits no privileges or specific gifts in man, save those won by his own Ego through personal effort and merit through a long series of Metempsychosis and Reincarnations."

Souls are reincarnated hundreds and thousands of times; but not the *person* (which implies the body), for the body perishes. These things were taught by the Essenes, Gnostics, Therapeutae and Jesus; and the doctrine is embodied in the parable of the Talents, as thus explained:—Into the soul of the individual is breathed the Spirit of God, divine, pure, and without blemish. It is God. And the individual has, in his earth-life, to nourish that Spirit and feed it as a Flame with Oil. When you put oil into a lamp, the essence passes into and becomes flame. So is it with the soul of him who nourishes the Spirit. It grows gradually pure, and *becomes* the Spirit. By this means the Spirit becomes the richer. And, as in the parable of the Talents, where God has given five talents, man pays back ten; or he returns nothing, and perishes.

When a soul has once become regenerate, it

returns to the body only by its own free will, and
as a Redeemer or Messenger. Such a one regains
in the flesh the memory of the past. Regeneration
or Transmutation may take place in an instant; but
it is rarely a sudden thing, and it is best that it
come gradually, so that the "Marriage" of the
Spirit be only after a prolonged engagement.

The doctrine of "Counterparts," so familiar to
certain classes of "Spiritualists," is a travesty, due
to delusive spirits, of the "Marriage of Regenera·
tion." Regeneration does not affect the interior
man only. A regenerated person may have his
body such that no poison will cause death. ("Za·
noni," in Lytton's story, "drinking the poisoned
wine.")

At death, a portion of the soul remains uncon·
sumed—Untransmuted, that is, into spirit. The
soul is fluid, and between it and vapor is this anal·
ogy. When there is a large quantity of vapor in a
small place it becomes condensed, and is thick and
gross. But when a portion is removed, the rest
becomes refined, and is rare and pure. So it is
with the soul. By the transmutation of a portion
of its material the rest becomes finer, rarer and
purer, and continues to do so more and more until
—after many incarnations, made good use of—the
whole of the soul is absorbed into the Divine Spirit,
and becomes one with God.

Every soul must *work out its own salvation*. Sal·
vation by Faith and the vicarious atonement were
not taught, as now interpreted, by Jesus, nor are
these doctrines taught in the exoteric Scriptures.

They are later and ignorant perversions of the original doctrines. In the Early Church, as in the Secret Doctrine, there was not one Christ for the whole world, but a *potential* Christ *in* every man. Theologians first made a fetish of the Impersonal Omnipresent Divinity; and then tore *Christos* from the hearts of all humanity in order to deify Jesus; that they might have a God-man peculiarly their own!

How much one's idea of God colors all his thoughts and deeds, is seldom realized. The ordinary crude and ignorant conception of a personal God more often results in slavish fear on the one hand, and Atheism on the other. It is what Carlyle calls "an absentee God, doing nothing since the six days of creation, but sitting on the outside and seeing it go!" This idea of God carries with it, of course, the idea of creation, as something already completed in time; when the fact is that creation is a process without beginning or end. The world—all worlds—are being "created" today as much as at any period in the past. Even the apparent destruction of worlds is a creative, or evolutionary process. Emanating from the bosom of the *all*, and running their cyclic course; day alternating with night, on the outer physical plane, they are again *indrawn* to the invisible plane, only to re-emerge after a longer night and start again on a higher cycle of evolution. Theologians have tried in vain to attach the idea of *immanance* to that of personality, and ended in a jargon of words and utter confusion of ideas. A personal Absolute is not, except in

potency. God does not *think*, but is the *cause* of
Thought. God does not love, He *is* Love, in the
perfect or absolute sense; and so with all the Divine
Attributes. God is thus the concealed Logos, the
"Causeless Cause." God never manifests Himself
(to be seen of men). Creation is His manifestation;
and as creation is not complete, and never will be,
and as it never had a beginning, there is a concealed
or unrevealed potency back of and beyond all creation, which is still God.

All men are brothers by all the laws of Nature
and by the very being of God. But so long as Religion defines Heresy as a crime, or imagines a God
with human attributes, "man's inhumanity to man"
will continue to make "countless millions mourn,"
and find vent for all evil passions justified by their
idea of God.

The Christ is no less Divine because all men may
reach the same Divine perfection. It will be urged
that "there is no other name given under heaven or
amongst men whereby we can be saved." This is
the Ineffable Name, which every Master is to possess and *become*, and salvation and perfection are
synonomous. Every act in the life of Jesus, and
every quality assigned to Christ, is to be found in
the life of Krishna and in the legend of all the Sun-
Gods from the remotest times.

That which the orthodox Christian will find to
oppose to this view is not that it dethrones or de-
grades Christ, but that it disproves the idea of
Christ as their exclusive possession, and denies
that all other religions are less Divine than their

own. The same selfishness is brought into religion
that is indulged in regard to other possessions,
such as wife and children, and other possessions
that are valued; and the same partisan spirit that
is in politics, and this more than anything else
appears to justify selfishness in general, militates
against the Universal Brotherhood of Man, and pre-
vents the founding of a Great Republic composed
of all nations and all people. This idea of Universal
Brotherhood was the cardinal doctrine in the Ancient Mysteries. There are no favorites in the
Divine Conception. Justice regards each individual
of all the myriads constituting Humanity with equal
favor. Justice of God toward all implies Justice
toward each other among men. This principle of
Justice is Law Universal, and this principle of
Brotherhood and the perfectibility of man's nature
through evolution necessitates Reincarnation. The
number of souls constituting Humanity, though
practically innumerable, is, nevertheless, definite.
Hence the doctrine of pre-existence taught in all
the Mysteries applied to "every child of woman
born; all conditions in each life being determined
by previous lives. (This is fully dealt with in
the "Beautiful Philosophy" by Count St. Vincent,
which is only open to Initiates.) Thus the Fatherhood of God in the personification of Divinity in
Humanity includes the Universal and Unqualified
Brotherhood of Man.

The real Masters in all ages, knowing this from
the lessons taught in the Mysteries of Initiation,
have ever been the foes of Autocrats, Oligarchies,

and Oppression in every form, whether ecclesiastical or Political. Initiates are taught to obey the laws of the country in which they live. They are not agents of Revolution, but of Evolution. By enlightenment and persuasion they may strive to reform a nation or a church. The true Republic is the outgrowth of Brotherhood, and a jealous monarch in Church or State will naturally oppose the diffusion of doctrines that tend to the liberation and enlightenment of the people.

Mysticism does not preach a new religion, it but reiterates the New Commandment announced by the Christ, which was also announced by every great reformer of religion since history began. Drop the theological barnacles from the Religion of Jesus, as taught by Him, and by the Essenes and Gnostics of the first centuries, and it becomes true Mysticism again. Mysticism or Occultism, is not derived from the Ancient Religion, Secret Doctrine of the Kabalah, but *is* the Secret Doctrine. Masonry and all other Orders founded on the Mysteries is derived from it and Mysticism is therefore *not* indebted to Masonry, but Masonry is indebted to Mysticism, because if it had not been for the Secret Doctrine, Masonry could not have existed, in fact, it would never have been founded.

The old Hebrew Kabalah as part of the Great Universal Wisdom-Religion of Antiquity, stands squarely for the Universal Brotherhood of Man, and has stood thus in all ages. To Christianize Mysticism or Occultism is an impossibility. It cannot be bound by any Creed or any Government; it is free.

"The thinnest veil over the Sublime Mystery of the Ineffable Name is Brotherhood and Love! The gross darkness that hangs like a black veil over the *Shekinah*, is Selfishness and Hate. Even so hath it ever been; and so will it ever be till Brotherly Love, Relief, and Truth reign universally in the hearts of all Humanity. The refinements of so-called Civilization do not change the essential nature of man. Beneath all these there sleeps or wakes a demon or an angel, and one of these is ever in chains, for no, man can serve two masters." Dr. J. D. Buck never wrote truer words than these.

The Science and Religion of the West are in perpetual conflict. The genius of this religion discerns Faith and Miracle as its foundation. Science holds as its ideals Fact and Law. Thus religion is necessarily illogical, while science is materialistic to the extreme, and, thanks to both, mankind is as far from any real knowledge of the nature and destiny of the soul as it was a thousand years ago. The, conflict has long been maintained; it is a war to the death; both religion and science are being reformed, and long before the battle ceases, *neither* of the original champions will be found to exist, except in their progeny of Eastern parentage.

The Western world laughs at this, for looking at the Secret Doctrine and the mighty religions of India, Egypt, Greece, and Judea only from the outside, nothing but discord, superstition, and chaos can be seen. But if one examines the symbols, questions the Mysteries, and searches out the root-idea of the founders and of the prophets, harmony

will be seen throughout. Along divers and often
winding paths, one will ever reach the same point,
so that penetration into the Arcanum of one of these
religions means entrance into the secrets of the
rest. Then a strange phenomena takes place. By
degrees, but in a widening circle, the Doctrine of
the Initiates is seen to shine forth in the Center of
the religions, like a Sun clearing away its nebula.
Each religion appears as a different planet. With
each we change both atmosphere and celestial ori-
entation, still it is always the same Sun which illu-
mines us. India, the mighty dreamer, plunges us
along with herself into the dream of eternity.
Egypt, sublime and imposing, austere as death, invites us to the journey, beyond the grave. Enchant-
ing Greece sweeps us along to the Magic feasts of
Life, and gives to her Mysteries the seduction of
her form, charming or terrible in turn, and of her
ever-passionate soul. Finally, Pythagoras scientifi-
cally formulates the Esoteric Doctrine, gives it the
most complete and concise expression it has ever
had. From these, then, will come our Science-Religion. The two in one.

The Western theory of Religion is that of a Personal God and an arbitrary and equally mechanical,
though miraculous creation; of a Revelation equally
miraculous; of souls created as by arbitrary caprice
of Deity, with the accidental co-operation of man,
even in violation of Divine Law. It talks of Laws,
but admits their abrogation through the Will (caprice) of God. It is true that neither Science nor
Religion has openly formulated the foregoing creeds,

but they are fair deductions from the postulates assumed, the logical results of a Nature without Intelligence; and a God who creates Laws only to annul them at his own good pleasure! Reconciliation between Science and Religion thus becomes impossible, because each is a contradiction to itself. How different this from the Doctrine taught by the Initiate Orpheus:

"*God* is one and eternally *unchangeable*. He reigns over all. *The Gods* are diverse and innumerable, for Divinity is eternal and infinite. The greatest are the souls of the constellations. Each constellation has its own suns and stars, earths and moons, and all issue from the *Celestial Fire* of Zeus, from the Initial Light. Half-conscious, inaccessible, and unchangeable, they govern the mighty whole by their unvarying movements. Each revolving constellation draws along in its ethereal sphere phalanxes of demi-gods or radiant souls who were formerly human, and who, after descending the scale of kingdoms, have gloriously ascended the cycles, and finally issued from the round of generations. It is through these divine spirits that God breathes, acts, and manifests himself; or, rather, these form the breath of His living soul, the rays of His eternal consciousness. They rule over armies of lower spirits which govern the elements; they control the universe.* Far and near, they surround us, and,

---

* Those who are on the Path and desire to know more of how things are ruled and brought about by the Masters, especially those of the Third Degree, should gain access to the Mss. "Beautiful Philosophy" by the Count St. Vincent. This Mss. is only to be had by Neophytes and Initiates.

although of immortal essence, they assume ever-
changing forms, according to nation, epoch or
region. The impious man who denies their existence still dreads them; the pious man worships
without knowing them; *the Initiate knows, attracts,
and sees them.* I struggled to find them, braved
death, and, as is said, descended into hell to tame
the demons of the abyss, to summon the gods from
on high to my beloved Greece, that lofty heaven
might unite with earth, listening with delight to
strains divine. Celestial beauty will become incar-
nate in the flesh of women, the *Fire* of Zeus will run
in the blood of heroes, and long before mounting to
the constellations the sons of the Gods will shine
forth like Immortals."

It will be seen that there is nothing Negative in
the Secret Doctrine, nor in the Doctrines of Krishna, Orpheus, Buddha and the other Gods. All they
taught was of a Positive nature. It is only in the
Western religion, which are mere forgeries of the
Eastern Doctrines that we find everything Negative.
A lie can never be Positive, because the positive
element is missing.

Krishna, an Initiate as mighty as Orpheus, taught
the doctrine of the immortal soul, its *rebirths* and
mystical union with God. The body, he taught,
envelopes the soul, which makes therein its dwelling, is a finished thing, but the indwelling soul is invisible, imponderable, incorruptible, eternal. This
latter became the doctrine of Plato. "The earthly
man is threefold, like the Divinity of which he is the
reflection: intelligence, soul and body. If the soul

is united with the intelligence it attains to *Sattva*—
Wisdom and Peace; if it remains uncertain, between
the intelligence and the body, it is dominated by
rajas—passion, and turns from object to object in a
fatal circle; if it abandons itself to the body it falls
into *tamas*—want of reason, ignorance, and temporary death.   This every man may observe in and
around himself.

"The soul never escapes the law, but always
obeys it.   This is the Mystery of Rebirths.   As the
depths of heaven are laid bare before the starry
rays, so the depths of life light up beneath the glory
of this truth.   When the body is dissolved, when
sattva is in the ascendant, the soul flies away into
the region of those pure beings who have knowledge of the Sublime.   When the body experiences
this dissolution whilst *rajas* dominates, the soul
once more comes to live amongst those who have
bound themselves to things of earth.   Again, if the
body is destroyed when *tamas* dominates, the soul,
whose radiance is dimmed by matter, is again
attracted by the wombs of irrational beings.

"The devout man, surprised by death, after
enjoying for several centuries the due reward of his
virtues in superior realms of bliss, finally returns
again to inhabit a body in some holy and respecta-
ble family.   But this kind of regeneration in this
life is very difficult to attain.   The man thus born
again finds himself possessed of the same degree
of application and advancement, as regards the
intellect, as he had in his first body, and he begins
to work afresh perfection in devotion."

"The mighty and profound secret, the sublime
and sovereign mystery, is that: To attain to perfection one must acquire *the knowledge of unity*, which
is above wisdom: one must rise to the divine Being
who is above the soul, above the intelligence.   This
divine Being, this sublime Friend *is in each one of us:
God dwells within each man, though few can find him:
This is the Path of salvation.*   Once thou hast perceived the perfect Being who is above the world and
within thyself, do thou decide to abandon the enemy,
which takes the form of desire.   Control thy passions.   The joys afforded by the senses are like
wombs of future sufferings.   Not only do good, *but
be good.*   Let the motive be in the action, not in its
fruits.   Adandon the fruits of thy works, but let
each action be as an offering to the Supreme being.
The man who sacrifices his desire and works to the
Being whence proceed the beginnings of all things,
and by whom the universe has been formed, attains
to perfection by this sacrifice.   One in spirit, he
acquires that spiritual wisdom which is above the
worship of offerings, and experiences a felicity
divine.   For he who *within* himself finds his happiness, his joy, and light, is one with God.   Know
then that the soul which has found God is freed
from rebirth and death, old age and grief.   Such a
soul drinks the waters of immortality."

Thus Krishna explained his doctrine, which was
really the Secret Doctrine of the Ancients, to his
disciples; by *inner* contemplation he gradually
raised them to the sublime truths which had been
opened out to himself in the lightning-flash of his
vision.

The old universal Wisdom Religion or Secret Doctrine is scientific to the last degree; for beneath both Science and Religion is the Philosophy which discerned the ordinary process of Eternal Nature, with no "missing links" in evolution, and no caprice or contradictions anywhere in Cosmos.   This is the Science-Religion that is being implanted in the Western world and as it grows, so will the so-called Science and Religion of the present day fade away.

The Perfect Man is Christ; and Christ is God. This is the birthright of every human soul.   It was taught in all the Greater Mysteries of Antiquity, but the Exoteric creeds of Christendom derived from the parables and allegories in which this doc- trine was concealed from the ignorant and the pro- fane, have accorded this Supreme Consummation to Jesus alone, and made it obscure to all the rest of humanity.   In place of this, the grandest doc- trine ever revealed to man, theologians have set up Salvation by Faith in a man-made Creed, and the Authority of the Church to "bind or loose on Earth or in Heaven." Law is annulled; Justice, dethroned; Merit, ignored; Effort discouraged; and Sectarian- ism, Atheism, and Materialism are the result.

All real Initiation is an internal, not an external, process. The outer ceremony is dead and useful only so far as it symbolizes and illustrates, and thereby makes clear the inward change.   In many of the Greater Orders, Ceremonial Initiation is entirely dispensed with, as it clouds, in many cases, the mind that would otherwise be clear.   In *true* Initiation no ceremonies are needed.   To Initiate truly, means to transform; to transform means to regenerate; and this comes only by trial, by effort, by *self*-conquest, by sorrow, disappointment, *failure;* and a daily renewal of the conflict.   It is in this that man must "work out his own salvation." The consummation of Initiation is the Perfect Master, the *Christos*, for these are the same.   They are the goal, the perfect consummation of human evolution.

By constant struggle and daily conflict the Master has conquered *self*.   Life after life he has gathered experience.   Truly hath he been a "man of sorrows and acquainted with grief."   He has assailed all problems; studied all science; exhausted all litanies; apprehended all Philosophies; practiced all arts.   At every step he has loved and helped humanity more and more, and sought his own desires less and less.   Grown familiar thus with all planes of life by sore trial, by bitter conflict, by frequent defeat, by hope deferred, almost despairing, he has at last renounced self utterly, and so became "dead to the world."

The Initiate of the highest grade—one who has power to command the elemental spirits, and thereby to hush the storm and still the waves—can, through the same agency, heal the disorders and regenerate the functions of the body.   And this he does by an exercise of his will which sets in motion the magnetic fluid.

Such a person, an Adept or Hierarch of magnetic srience, is, necessarily, a person of many Incarnations.   And it is principally in the East that these

are to be found. For it is there that the oldest
souls are wont to congregate. It is in the East that
human Science first arose; and the soil and astral
fluid there are charged with power as a vast battery
of many piles. So that the Hierarch of the Orient
both is himself an older soul and has the magnetic
support of a chain of older souls, and the earth beneath his feet and the medium around him are
charged with electric force to a degree not to be
found elsewhere. It is for this reason that the East
is far more enlightened than the West.

How can man become such a Master according
to the Doctrine? The man who is without fear and
without concupiscence; who has courage to be absolutely poor and absolutely chaste. When it is all
one to you whether you have gold or whether you
have none, whether you have a house and lands or
whether you have them not, whether you have
worldly reputation or whether you are an outcast,
—then you are voluntarily poor. It is *not* necessary to have nothing but it is necessary to care for
nothing. When it is all one to you whether you
have a wife or husband, or whether you are a celi-
bate, then you are free from concupiscence. It is
not necessary to be a virgin; it is necessary to set
no value on flesh. There is nothing so difficult to
attain as this equilibrium—the Double Triangle.
The White interlaced with the Black. When you
have ceased both to wish to retain and to burn, then
you have the remedy in your hands, and the remedy
is hard and a sharp one, and a terrible ordeal.
Nevertheless, be thou not afraid. Deny the five

senses, and above all the taste and the touch. The power is *within* you if you will to attain it. Eat no dead thing. Drink no fermented drink. Make living elements of all the elements of your body. Take your food full of life, and let not the touch of death pass upon it. Remember that without self-immolation there is no power over death.

When a man has attained power over the body, the process of ordeal is not longer necessary. The Initiate is under a vow; the Hierarch is Free. Jesus, therefore, came eating and drinking; for all things were lawful to him. He had undergone, while a Neophyte with the Essenes, and had freed his will. For the object of the trial and the vow is polarisation. When the fixed is volatliised, the Magian is free. But before Christ was Christ he was subject; and his Initiation lasted thirty years. All things are lawful to the Hierarch; for he knows the nature and value of all.

By evolution man is continually climbing upward to higher planes. His five senses are adjusted to observations and experiences of the physical plane; but he has other experiences. The senses are narrow and circumscribed; yet even these become refined. His tastes alter, his tendencies ascend. He is reaching outward as his sympathies expand, and upward, as his ideals become higher. There is revealed to him a whole world of experience in which the lower senses play no part; a world of aspiration in which Self is *not* the goal. The very physical bounds of self are loosening, expanding, and disappearing. Hitherto he has been conscious

6

of flashes in intuition; of knowing things he has
seemingly never learned.   He sees *inner* meanings,
and senses subtler powers.   Not only in visions and
intuitions of the day, but in dreams of the night he
has experiences beyond the bounds of sense.   He
learns the power of Thought.   By conquering Self,
his Will becomes strong.   By subduing passion,
his mind becomes clear.   He has premonitions of
coming events; for all events and thoughts and
things exist first on higher planes, and are precipi-
tated thence into matter.   He becomes clairaudient
and clairvoyant.   He has broken the bonds of Self
and now functions on higher planes.   As his senses
and organs on the physical plane made him Master
there of brutes, and of physical nature, even so
on the higher plane, the senses and organs evolve
by the same Evolutionary Law of experience and
choice, make him, on the higher plane, Master of
men and of Higher Nature.

The problem of genuine initiation, or training in
Occultism, consists in placing all the operations of
the body under the dominion of the Will; in freeing
the Ego from the dominion of the appetites, passions,
and the whole lower nature.   The idea is not to de-
spise the body, but to purify it: Not to destroy the
appetites, but to elevate and control them absolutely.
This mastery of the lower nature does not change
the Key of the physical nature as such; but subor-
dinates it to that of a higher plane.   Without this
subordination, the clamorous lower nature drowns
out all higher vibrations: as if in an orchestra, the
bass-viols and the drums only could be heard; and
noise rather than harmony would result.

The first point to be made in real Initiation is for the Thinker to control his thoughts. Instead of passively and helplessly receiving all suggestions that come from the physical sense, or appetites; or all that come from ambition, selfishness and pride; he selects, and chooses, and Wills what thoughts shall come. In this manner he acquires mastery over his own mind, and frees his will from the dominion of Desire; or rather elevates and purifies Desire.

In the Ancient Mysteries not every Initiate became a Master. There were the Lesser and the Greater Mysteries. To the Lesser all were eligible; to the Greater, very few; and of these few, fewer still were ever exalted to the sublime and last degree. Some remained for a lifetime in the lower degrees, unable to progress further on account of the constitutional defect or mental and spiritual incapacity. Thus it is now. The Mysteries unfolded the Building of Worlds, the Religion of Nature, the Universal Brotherhood of Man, the Immortality of the Soul, and the Evolution of Humanity. No ceremony was artificial and meaningless; no symbol, however grotesque to the ignorant, was merely fanciful.

Thales and Pythagoras learned in the Sanctuaries of Egypt that the Earth revolved around the Sun, but they did not attempt to make this generally known, because to do so would have been necessary to reveal one of the great Secrets of the Temple, the double law of attraction and radiation, or of sympathy and antipathy, or of fixedness and movement, which is the principle of creation and the perpetual cause of life. The truth was ridiculed by Lactanius, as it was long after sought to be proven a falsehood by persecution of Papal Rome.

The Ideal in Church and State, the *motive* for the Ecclesiastical and Political Hierarchies, has been in all ages to govern men professedly for their own good. The Secret Doctrine teaches man to govern himself. So long as Hierarchies subordinate all things to the real benefit of man, and give Light and Knowledge to *all* in such measure as they can receive, they are a blessing and not a curse. When, however, the Potentiate suppresses Knowledge, claims power by Divine Right, or by inheritance, rather that by proof of knowledge and by service done to man; when ignorance or disbelief is punished as a crime and men torture the body, or agonize the mind under the devil's plea---"to save the soul"--- then does the Hierarchy become an enemy of both God and Man. Freedom and Enlightenment are the only real Saviors of Mankind; while ignorance is the father of Superstition, and Selfishness the parent of Vice.

The Ancient Mysteries were organized schools of learning, and knowledge was the signal of progress and the basis of Fellowship. The doors of real Initiation were open to women as to men. Such is the case at the present time. The Illuminati and the Rosicrucians both admit women to their Initiation on equal footing with men. Masonry at one time also admitted them until the Fraternity was betrayed by her. Since then she has been excluded.

The time will come again when Masonry will put aside most of its Ceremonialism and teach the pure Secret Doctrine, then will women again be admitted as of yore.

The Ancient Wisdom concerned itself largely, as it does at present, with the Souls of men, and undertook to elevate the earthly life by purifying the Soul and exalting its Ideals. It teaches that souls are sexless; and that the sex of the body is an incident of gestation. No civilization known to man has ever risen to any great heights, or long maintained its supremacy, that debased woman. The Secret Doctrine demonstrates with unmistakable clearness that sexual debasement in any form is the highway of degeneracy and destruction of both man and woman; and of Nations quite as certainly as of individuals.

Ever since the time of Atlantis, the *true* Adepts and Masters have been the keepers of the Great Lodge. These Masters have taught the Secret Religions and true Science. The ancient governments were Partiarchal; (See History of Atlantis by Dr. Phelon) the Ruler was also a Master Initiate, and the people were regarded as his children. In those days a Reigning Prince did not consider it beneath his dignity to go into the desert alone, and sit at the feet of some inspired recluse, in order that he might receive more light, which he would dispense to those that were ready to receive such teachings. Instead of teaching superstition and idolatry, when the real meaning of symbolism is revealed, it will be found to be the thinnest veil ever imposed between the sublime Wisdom and the apprehension of men. The old gods were the symbolical or personified attributes of Nature, through which man was taught to apprehend the existence of the Supreme Spirit. This was not Polytheism, nor idolatry, but a system of teaching that which could not be altogether defined, and of pointing to that which must forever remain unknown, and Unknowable, by the aid of symbol, parable, and allegory. No word painting known to man seems half so beautiful as some of these ancient parables and allegories. Not only was every oblation to love and duty portrayed, and every joy of home and affection illustrated, and the most common duties of life, feats of valor, devotion, and self-sacrifice depicted, but in a language so musical, and in rhythm and meter so perfect, as to make the whole recital more like a symphony than a poem.

The parables were *not* invented to conceal the truth from those who could apprehend it, or to keep the people in ignorance in order that the Priests or Ruler might preserve their power, for no Initiate cares for power except that he may do good to humanity. No Initiate seeks to control any people or office, the people seek the Initiate. "We seek no man, but man seeks us." Power came not from the people but from the possession of supreme knowledge, and this knowledge, continually exercised and exemplified, was the badge of office and the sign of authority. To such a Priesthood the people rendered most willing obedience. The doors of Initiation were open, then as at this time, to all who had evolved the capacity to "Know, to Dare to Do, and to Keep Silent," in regard to that which should not be prematurely revealed.

With the Light of the Great Lodge standing in the midst, the Religion of the people was a perfect representative of Science and Philosophy, in which superstition and idolatry found no place, hence the symmetry in all the Old Wisdom Religions. There was really but one Secret Doctrine, but in later times, many Nations had the same Philosophy, but each Nation has its own Grand Supreme Lodge.

The religions of Egypt and Chaldea, as has been stated, had back of them the same Secret Doctrine, or Mysteries; as had been taught in the Great Lodge of Atlantis, for it was from there that they were transplanted to Egypt, India, Asia and other coun-tries. This religion was both Scientific and Philo-sophical. Egypt and Chaldea repeated the folly of India, and perished, with the exception of a few Initiates who remained true, with the degradation of their religion. The few who remained true to their vows kept the Secret Doctrines in the Secret Archives of the Temples and Masters like Hermes, Zoroaster, Confucius, and others were secretly taught the Secret Doctrines and revived the old religion under new names, and often under a dif-ferent form of symbolism. Pythagoras and the Schools of the Persian Magi for many centuries kept the true light burning and it could always be found by those who were truly seeking for it.

The conquest of Egypt by Cambyses completed the ruin of the land of Pharaohs, and Pythagoras

and Plato became the links between the old philosophy and the Christian Mysteries, together with
the Jewish Kabalah, derived jointly from the Mysteries of Atlantis, Egypt and Asia.

From the Essenes, the Schools of Alexandria
then in all their glory, from the Kabalah and the
philosophy of Plato, the Christian Mysteries were
derived. In fact, the Christian Mysteries were
none other than the Ancient Mysteries or Secret
Doctrine, but became known as the Christian Mysteries after the Initiation of Christ by the Essenes.
During the first three centuries of the present era
these doctrines flourished openly; but were finally
forced to be taught secretly through the conquest
of Constantine, and then came the dark ages for
the people.

The Religion of Jesus was therefore that of the
Mysteries; it was the same Wisdom-Religion,
though perhaps the ethical features were more
pronounced, as being needed among what was called
"a generation of vipers." The ethical teachings of
Jesus in time gave place to Priest-craft and Sacer-
dotalism; to worldly power, and conquest; and the
religion, or rather, ceremonialism of Constantine
was finally succeeded by the "Holy Inquisition," a
religion of torture and bloodshed. History is full
of pretenders in Occultism and Mysticism. Pre-
tension alone is a sign of ignorance, and the propo-
sition to "sell the truth" is always a sign of fraud.
"Every man is worthy of his hire," the teacher
must be paid for his work. The publisher for his
books, but for the teachings no price can be paid

in current coin.   There are many names in history
that have been covered with obloquy, and their pos-
sessors charged with fraud and imposition, who
were genuine Adepts.   The seeker should distinguish between self-conviction that comes from the
pretender's own mouth and those accusations that
come from others and are unsupported by evidence.
As a fact, the true Master or Initiate, never, under
any circumstances, makes the claim that he is
such.   *The man or woman that openly claims to be
either an Initiate, an Adept, or a Master, is never
such, but is simply a pretender.*   The pretender is
usually loaded with honors and found rolling in
wealth, as the reward of deceit and lying, of fraud
and corruption, which he is shrewd enough to
conceal from the masses but which he can never
hide from an Initiate or Master.   Man betrays his
character, his heredity, his ideas, and all his past
life in every lineament of his face, in the pose of his
body, in his gait, in the lines of his hands, in the
tones of his voice and in the expression of his eye
especially.   No man possesses character.   Character is that which he *is*, and not something apart
from himself.   One need not be a Master to discover all this; he needs only to observe, to think,
and to reason on what he sees.   The individual who
is really sincere and devout will not fail to recognize
sincerity and true devotion in an acquaintance or in
any character in history that possessed these virtues.   Hence the Student of the Sacred or Occult
Science, though not himself an Adept, learns to
recognize by unfailing signs those in the present

or past who were really Masters and who knew
the True Wisdom.

The *real* Master is often gibbeted by the populace
and anathematized by the church, because he is
neither time-serving nor willing to barter the truth
for gold.

All along the line of history, from the foundation
of Atlantis to the present time, may be found those
who possessed the *true Light*.   Masters who concealed both their Wisdom and their own identity
from vulgar notice and foolish praise, they walked
the earth in the past as now, unseen and unknown
to the many, but always known to their fellows,
and to all real seekers after true wisdom.

These Adepts, or Masters, have, in every age, as
at the present time, constituted the Great Lodge.
They were, and are, the Masters of the Fraternities.   *For be it known to all those who would find the
Light, to all those who would trod the Path, these Great
Lodges exist to-day as they did in the past and Initiates
know that there are more real Masters to-day than ever
before.*   Whether they congregate beneath vaulted
domes, or meet at stated times, no one would be
likely to know unless he belongs to the same degree;
but one thing is very certain, and that is, that they
help and bring knowledge to the world when most
needed and often shape the destinies of Nations.
They are working to-day in the West as they have
never done before.   They are enabled to work now,
because the ground has been prepared for them by

---

*See the "Beautiful Philosophy of Initiation" by Count St. Vincent,
for full information concerning this point.

"He who *knows*," and Masonry, although it has lost the Key to its own Mysteries, has done much to bring this about. How much more could Masonry do should it find the Key to its Mysteries? Truly, no one would be able to guess.

Fire-Philosophy

———

The Foundation of all True Initiation and all Mystic and Occult Fraternities, as well as the Secret Doctrine and the Ancient Mysteries.

———

OF all the Secret Orders, there is probably more known concerning the Fraternities of the Rosy Cross than of any other Order. This is not because the Fraternity itself has given so much of its teachings to the profane world, but on account of the writings of Hargrave Jennings, Paschal Beverly Randolph, Lord Bulwer Lytton, Honore de Balsac, Freeman B. Dowd and others. In one of the Manifestoes issued in the year 1871, by the then Supreme Master of the Fraternity---Dr. P. B. Randolph, it is admitted that the very foundation of the Fraternity is the Philosophy of *Fire*. He says:

" .... It is urged against us that we 'Believe in, and Practice Magic;' we admit the fact: we certainly *do*,---the pure white, bright, effulgent, radiantly glorious *Magic of the Human Will*,---through and by which *alone*, human passions are made to correct themselves, and by which *alone*, otherwise defenseless Woman is fully armed against the coarse brutality of thousands of misnamed 'men and husbands;' and this is a purely *Christic* power too, an integrant of the early Christic faith,---dead here, and buried nearly everywhere else, beneath mountains of gabble-dust, deserts of error. It is further charged that we have 'certain quite extraordinary Esoteric, or Secret Doctrines.' We admit the fact, and the animus is apparent from that other fact, namely, 'that these Secret Doctrines are only divulged to the pure, virtuous, and worthy.' Our assailants *failed* in all their schemes to penetrate these Mysteries, and the inference is plain, nor can even the disaffected fail to see 'the reason why!' Now, however, we herewith present some of these 'Secret Doctrines.'" . . . . .

Holding as we do, that Deity dwells *within* the cryptic portals of the luminous worlds, *and that the lamp that lights it is Love Supreme.*

We hold that no *power* ever comes to man through the intellect . . . . That Goodness alone is Power, and that *that* pertains to the *heart* only, hence that Power comes only to the Soul through *Love* (not lust, mind you, but *Love*), the underlying, Primal *Fire-Life*, sub-tending the bases of Being,—the formative flowing floor of the worlds,—the true *sensing* of which is the beginning of the road to personal power. *Love* lieth at the foundation, and is the synonym of life and strength and clingingness. . . .

Holding, as we do, that Deity dwells *within* the Shadow, *behind* the everlasting *Flame*,—the amazing glories of *which* minds have confounded with the very God,—we declare All *things, especially the human Soul, to be a form of Fire:* that man is *not* the only intelligence in nature, but that there are, and the aerial spaces abound with, multiform intelligences, having their conscious origin in *Aeth*, as man has his in matter; and that there are *grades* of these, towering away in infinite series of hierarchies, human, and ultra-human, to an unimaginable Eterne. We hold that the soul is a polar world of *White Fire within* the human body; that its *negative* only resides within the brain as a general dwelling; that in *dreamless* sleep it goes to the solar plexus to impart stores of *Life-Fire* to the body; in dream it visits (by sight and rapport) other scenery, and that all dreams have a determinate meaning and purpose. . . . .

We hold that the other pole of the soul is situated *within* the genital system. . . . . The superior pole of the soul is in direct magnetic and Ethereal contact with the Soul of Being; the *foundation-Fire* of the Universe; with all that vast domain underlying increase, growth, emotion, beauty, power, heat, energy; the *sole* and base of being, the subtending *Love*, or *Fire-floor* of Existence. Hence through Love man seizes directly on all that is, and is in actual contact and rapport with all and singular every being that *feels* and *Loves* within the confines of God's habitable universe. . . . .

" . . Declaring that true manhood is more or less en rapport with one or more of the Upper Hierarchies of Intelligent Potentialities, earth-born and *not* earth-born, *we believe there are means whereby a person may become associated with, and receive instructions from them.* More than that; we believe in talismans; that it is possible to construct and wear them, and that they emit a peculiar light, discernable across the gulfs of Space by these intelligent powers, just

as we discern a diamond across a playhouse; that
such signals to the beholders, and that they will,
and do cross the chasmal steeps to save, succor,
and assist the wearers, just as a good brother here
flies to the relief of him who shall give the grand
hailing-signs of distress. . . . .

" . . God, the Soul of the Universe, is *positive heat*,
Celestial Fire; the aura of Deity (God-od) is *Love*, the
prime element of all power, the external *Fire*-sphere,
the informing and formative pulse of matter. The
induction is crystalline; for it follows that whoso
hath most love.---whether its *expression* be coarse
or fine, cultured or rude,---hath, therefore, most of
God in him or her; the element of time being com-
petent to the perfection of all refining influences
over the ocean, if not upon the hither side. . . ."

From the quotations made of the Rosicrucian
Manifesto, it will be plain to the student that the
Fire-Philosophy is the very foundation of the Fraternity which was founded in the Temple of Atlantis and has continued, under various names, up to
the present time.   An Rosicrucian says:---

"Justice is so late of arrival to all original think-
ers---the terms of prejudice, and of astonishment
(not in the good sense), are so long in falling off
from profound researches---that even now, the
Rosicrucians---in other words, the Paracelsians or
Magnetists---are totally ignored as the arch-chem-
ists, to whose deep thoughts, and unrelaxing labors,
modern science is indebted for most of its truths.

As astrology (not the juggles of the stars, but the
true exploration, seeking the method of being, and

of working, of the glittering habitants of space):
as astrology was the mother of astronomy, so is
the lore of the Hermetic Brethren (miscalled in
only one of their names—and that the popular
Rosicrucians)—the groundwork of all present
philosophy.   On its applied side, Rosicrucianism is
the very science which is so familiar and so valuable.
But as the Hermetic (Rosicrucian) Beliefs are a
great religion, they of course, have their popular
adaptations; and, in consequence, there is a mythology to them.   There must always be a machinery
(symbolism) to every faith, through which it may
be known; and the mistake of people is in accepting
the childish machinery and the coarse (but fitly)
colored mythology of a religion for the religion
itself, and all of it."

"Mystical, fantastical, and transcendental—nay,
impossible—as the studies and objects of the Rosicrucians seem in these modern, ultra-practical
days, it is forgotten that the truths of contemporan-
eous science are all based on the dreams of the old
thinkers.   Out of natural philosophy, the occult
brethren sought the spirits of natural philosophy,
and to this *inner* heaven—so unlike ordinary life—
through purifications, through invocations, through
humbling and prayers, through penances to break
the terms of body with the world, through fumiga-
tions and incensing to rise up another world about
them, and to place themselves *en rapport* with the
inhabitants of it, through the suspension of the
senses, and thereby to the opening of other senses
—to the shutting-out of one state, in order to the
7

passing into another state,—to all this the Rosicrucians sought to reach."

What is now known as Hermetic Doctrine is but a part of the Rosicrucian system, a branch of that Fraternity. Their teachings concerning Fire are identical with the Rosicrucian Doctrine concerning same. There is but a slight difference in the foundation of these Orders and that difference is to be found in their doctrine of "Conservation of Energy," according to their teachings: "Fire is at once the great purifier and separator of elements. It is hell for devils, but on the pure spirit it works no injury. For pure spirit is also the spirit of the *Fire*. The whole world must be purified by *Fire* or the intensity of true Love for the new dispensation. When we recall the fact that *Pure Spirit* is also *Love*, we see what love really is, and will be to us and the whole world.

"Like all other things he touches, the undeveloped man has constantly acted to draw down everything belonging to the higher conception of sex. He forgets it is the *direct* emanation of the Divine creative thought. All the highest, purest, and sweetest thought leads up to the manifestation of the sex condition and sex forces, as the Alpha and Omega of both desire and fulfillment. It holds within itself, the whole Divine statement of Being: "and God said: Let there be and there was." In it there are life and death; the out-putting and in-drawing."

"All the great lessons of living and acting are held in this three-lettered word of unperfected activity.   The Law of Love—God expression in man, holds its basis of manifestation on the health activity of the sex function.   The beginning and the end of life, if we so will it, is held here.   The moment of conclusion is the beginning of life.   It is also the moment of death—the dead point at which the whole organism enters into the realms of dissolution, as it is ever striving to do.   But the great sex-force and body of life carries always *forward and beyond*, so there shall be no dwelling *within* the House of Death.

"It is in this '*House of the Fire of Life*' wherein is manifested the completion of the Divine plan.   It is there the Was becomes the Is, and the *is—is* passes into the Shall Be.   It is through this differentiation, that the great trinity manifests itself unto itself.   Verily, the kingdom of Heaven—the Power of God—lies *within* us, for the Transmission of Life.   His knowledge of its origin is the point, at which His Supremacy assumes for itself unquestioned authority—the Omnipotence of the One only Unity.   *Love, Sex*, and *Fire* are one.   The Three in One.'"

At the present day in Sweden, on the first of May—the opening or germination of the the year—the peasantry, as they do all over the North at certain times, light fires.   A candle is lighted by all devout Catholics on Christmas Eve, and is kept burning, in memory and reminder of the mysterious Incarnation, until the dawning of the real day.

---

*See, "Divine Alchemy."

of the Blessed Nativity. The Yule-Log, whose bright blazing is of so much moment, and with the last brand of which, most carefully and superstitiously laid aside for the purpose, the next year's Christmas *Fire* is to be lighted, follows the same rule. The Christmas Tree, the origin of which is lost in the mists of tradition, and which Teutonic emblem (time out of mind employed in Germany) is now transposed into England, though without the slightest suspicion of its Pagan meaning, is the Mystic Northern sacrifice, and the attestation, in its multitudinous blazing candles, to the Genius or God of the *Fire*. The toys representing all the things of man, and of the earth, which are suspended among the boughs, in its mystic light, are the sacrifice of all the good things of the world, and all the products of the Creative Fiat, as in surrender and acknowledgement, back to the Unknown Living Spirit, or Immortal Producer, who hath chosen *Fire* as his symbol and his shadow.

"If the reader will refer to the crest of His Royal Highness Prince Albert, he will find the Mystic, Magic horns distinctly set up. The reproduction of the ever-recurring symbol which is recognizable as horns, wings, or otherwise in the head-pieces of his ancestors of the North. The rough Runic Soldiers who, in their barbarian incursions, overturned (in the Roman beliefs), and buried in the ruins of the Empire, a faith identical, in its secrets, with their own. All-ignorant of the fact that the symbols of both spoke but the same tale, the original, Magic, Fire-Faith.

"The laurel-wreath around the head of heroes and emperors—accorded alone to the great conquerers, the Imperator, or the poet (majestic Triplicate!), not only mark out the line, and denote the place of the organs of the highest intellectual and god-like faculties in the brows of the human being, but prove the knowledge of the ancients of phrenology, and represent the original starry *radius*—that which symbolically invests the head of all the Gods. It speaks the *Spirit Flame* or *radius*—magnetic and supernatural—intensifying to its real magico-generative power in a circle of intolerable light, about the head: in which Mystic Light all Magic and sorcery, as well as all Sainthood, was supposed, by the Rosicrucians, to be possible, in accordance with the laws of the super-natural Fire-World. Crowns, garlands, wreaths, all the *insignia* of dignity that encircle the head; and all passing, be it remarked, over the physico-phrenological places of the faculties of "causality, comparison, wonder, and imagination," and in tracing them along, disclosing and glorifying all the bodily points of the means of the greatness of man,—mitres and priestly head coverings, the tonsure of the sacredotes, freeing the sacred circle of the intellect (within which may the terrifically grand, very apprehension of God, himself, be realized): from the barbarian and the degraded—nay, brute-like growth of hair, the very investiture and most closely branding confession, and the complete and irresistible conviction, of the beasts—most abundant, and the grossest, there were, in the scale, lowest;—sceptres, wands, priest-

7I

ly staves or crosiers, batons and maces:—all these
marks of rank, with the original disk, orb, mound,
surmounting, with the Mystic symbol of the Cross,
the royal rods or sceptres of the European monarchs:—*all these forms are but the changes and reproduction of the rod of the Magician. He whose creed was
the Fire-creed, and whose secret means of working upon
nature was the mysterious "Sorcerer's Sign," displayed
upon, and through which stretched—he declared—the
"shows" of the worlds, and converse with the real Sub-
strata of which, he pronounced, was by spells, as spirit-
visages were only to be won to the sight, or through en-
chantments.*

It has already been shown that both Krishna and
Orpheus taught the Christian Mysteries.   Buddha,
another founder of Religion, also taught these Mysteries and the Secret Doctrine, and Buddhism is
nothing short of Fire Philosophy.

"The subject of Buddhism is the obscurest in the
whole round of learned inquisition."   Says Hargrave Jennings: "This old, and (beyond all measure) the broadest and the sublimest of *all* the religions of the East;—this ancient and really philosophical belief—demands a capacity to grasp abstractions before its principles can be understood.
Men who argue from effect to cause—men who apprehend cause at all—that is, cause as gathered
from an experience derivable from being;—cannot
but fail in attaining to the disclosure of it.   Materialism is a constant charge urged upon the Buddhist.   In one sense, materialism is correctly assured of him.   For Buddhism denounces all being,

apart from form, as impossible. It is the purest
Spinozism. It is identical with it. As all forms
of true philosophy—whether Grecian, Egyptian,
Eastern—all that rest upon a truth that, in this
sense is truer than nature,—must rest upon Spinozism. . . . .

"Accepted with the literal eye, the tenets of the
Indian theology, in reference to its Buddhist ground-
work, appear to present the usual average of myth-
ologic fabling. But *we* judge upon the means of expression, *not* upon the thing expressed. That, in
the very terms of expression, has escaped. As the
reconcilement of that which 'knows no sense,' with
apprehension through the means of sense alone,
must always be impossible. Man's very being—
that is the laws by which he is, or his mind, shut
him up, as it were, *within* themselves (or itself), as
in a prison. And all his knowledge of things comes
from that Light shining *within* his prison—his mind.
Within that radius, the Light is perfect and he himself perfect. But what guesses he, or can he know,
of the great Light without? That light, to him,
may be no light. Light is material. Being, itself,
only necessary to matter, and the life of it, or the
soul of the world.

"So taught the Persian believers in the one Universal groundwork of light—the soul, or ultimate
principle of everything to be known—which is the
religion of the Magi, of Zoroaster, of the Guebres,
of the modern Indian Parsees as of the middle age
European Bohemians; the remains of whose Fire-
Palaces, or Fire-Temples, are yet to be seen, crumb-

ling, indeed, into their own god, *light*, around the reverend and time-battered, as well as war battered, **Prague.**

"Man is the center to himself in his light of mind, shining as in his castle and prison of body. The forceful outer day ··· the god of the universal circle of things ···once, in its violent inquest, fixed of a cranny and penetrating, would annihilate the temporary possessor of the tenement, and absorb all *within* (that is, him), to itself···laws to light; organism to broad being. Until reincorporate; that is concrete.

"The whole round world is as a microcosm, whose wonders are exhaustless; whose beauties are beyond expression; whose changes, whose decay, whose recommitment into new forms is as the ceaseless revolvement of the Inexpressible Glory. Through the sea floors and their multitudinous mimic continents, fruitful of moving life, fecund with their tree-growths and their semi sylvan, semi-oceanic vegetation; through the clouds of the seas that rest or roll over them, through which speed the winged ships as golden (sunlighted) specks; through the hollow-crusted earth and its rigid rocks ···earth torn and battered like a battle-beaten man of Eternal War, as it circles its resounding way amidst the roads of the lighted stars, 'baring' to the changing Sun, and to the cold, renewing moon, its ploughed side, globing up, still defiant, with the wounds of the contentions of the centuries and with the retardation of the space-forces;···through the 'built-work' of Nature, in short runs the ever coursing Inner Spirit, which forces, in its stupendous track (comet-like) the bordering matter into *Flame* ---to *Life*.

"Is not all the world a woven tissue---wizard-colored---of which the creative sun strikes the spangles into sparkling; stains, prismatically, with the rose-hues of being, or the blues of decay---or, rather, change? Roars not old ocean with his caves; as the Nereid music swelleth or sinketh, to fascination, loudly or faintly through its shell? Fires, and smokes, and springs, and steam attest the attenuate bulk, spun through the hands of the Great Magnetic Life, or by the power of the Earth-God, into tissues. What is as the core, and the mighty heart of the great world, but the spouting *Fire?* What are the magnificent air-shapes of our atmosphere; what the crossed cloud-platforms of our sky; what the reduplicate and multiplicate fog-work and flocculence of the Western or the Eastern Heavens, when the golden or the burning light is poured through the heaped wonder-worlds of the Magician of the Great Air;---what should be all the *cloud-settings* or our sky, but as the precipitate, and dress, of the mere 'used-up-matter;'---glorious to our senses, as even all the *refuse* is? And if *Fire* be, in its own nature---so to speak---but the roaring-back, *Illuminate*, of Nature from the real unto the unreal (*as which the Magi teach, and as which the worshippers of the element of Fire believe*), then the very excess of material light shall be but as the very *excess* of the dense matter, remonstrating (as it were), itself the brighter as it is, in itself, the blacker. Nor are these the vagaries of Philosophers, but the world-old persuasions, when the vanity of knowledge had not made a base 'machine of wheels' of the world!

"Let us rest with this sublime assurance. That the Kingdom of God lieth much nearer to us than consists in our vain imagination of possibilities. Yea, is at our door! God on our Threshold! We all the while---Peter-like---denying him. Denying the Spirits because we cannot feel the Spirit!"

"The Old Buddhists---as equally as the ancient believers in the Doctrine of the Universal Spiritual Fire---held that Spirit Light was the floor or basis of all created things. The material side or complement of this Spiritual Light being *Fire*, into which element all things could be rendered; and which (or Heat) was the motive of all things that are. They taught that matter or mind---as the superflux---as the sum of sensations, or as natural and unreal shows of their various kinds---were piled, as layer on layer, or tissue on tissue, on this immutable and Immortal floor or ground-work of Divine *Flame*, the soul of the World.

Such is the magnificent view of the Buddhists of Creation. Is it any wonder that it has more votaries than any other system of Religion? *Fire, Love---God*, is the foundation of this Philosophy, as of all other true Philosophies and it is for this reason that it must endure forever, until Universal Brotherhood is a fact.

The emotion, intensity, mind-agitation, thought, according to the powers of the unit or the lifting heavenward:---or as the dots or dimples in the ever-flowing onwave of being: were---to speak in the familiar sense---"as impressions down," perhaps through and through its covers, upon this living floor of Spiritual *Flame*. The escape of which was the magnetism---magnetism of the body: supersential force, or miracle, of the spirit.

"The Paracelsists or Theosophists of the sixteenth century were also Fire-Philosophers and were known as such. Theosophy we have at the present day although their teachings may be slightly changed at this time.

"The Fire-Philosophers, or *Philosophi per ignem*, were a sect of Philosophers who appeared towards the close of the sixteenth century. They were known throughout every country of Europe and declared that the intimate Essenes of natural things were only to be known by the trying effects of Fire, directed in a chemical process. The Theosophists, also, insisted that human reason was a dangerous and deceitful guide; that no real progress could be made in knowledge, or in religion, by it, and that to all vital, that is, supernatural purpose, it was a vain thing, they taught that Divine and supernatural exaltation was the only means of arriving at Truth.* Their name of Paracelsists was derived from Paracelsus,** the eminent physician and chemist, who was the chief Philosopher of this sect. In England, Robert Fludd was their great advocate

---

*See the " Beautiful Philosophy of Initiation."

** After the " Fama Fraternitatis ; or a Discovery of the Fraternity o the most Laudable Order of the Rosy Cross " was issued by Christian Rosencrutz, they became known as Rosicrucians. See " The Rosicrucians ; their Teachings,"

and exponent.   Rivier, who wrote in France; Severi-
nus, an author of Denmark; Kunrath, an eminent
physician of Dresden; and Daniel Hoffman, profes-
sor of Divinity in the University of Helmstadt, have
also treated largely on Paracelsus, and on his system.

"Akin to the school of the Ancient Fire Believers,
and of the Magnetists of a later period," says Dr.
Ennermoser, "of the same cast as these speculators
and searchers into the mysteries of nature, drawing from the same well, are the Theosophists of the
sixteenth and seventeenth centuries.   These practiced chemistry, by which they asserted that they
could explain the profoundest secrets of nature.
As they strove, above all earthly knowledge, after
the divine, and sought the *Divine Light* and *Fire*,
through which all men can acquire the true wisdom,
they were called the Fire-Philosophers.   As a great
general principle, the Theosophists called the Soul
a *Fire*, taken from the eternal ocean of Light."

Hargrave Jennings, the Rosicrucian and Philosopher, says: "We may thus sum our historical examination.   That, at every turn of our inquiry, we
meet Light.   At every cross-road, as it were, of
our laborious journey—of our philosophical pilgrimage --- we encounter this pertinacious and ever-
following Light.   Not only at birth, but as taking a
prominent part in the torch-celebration at marriage,
and again, and more impressively, at death and in
the ceremonials of sepulture, the panthom of Light
never fails.   It is the more dimly or the brighter ---
the more gloriously and the more cheerfully celeb-

rant, or the more awfully full everywhere disclosed.
As everything, it must---though disguised---be
everything? What may mean this concentrate,
Resplendent Fifure? This ever-following myth?
This terrible, and yet this Grand Angel, found at
the couch-side at our bith, accompanying us, as the
best and most distant sacrifice, to the altar of pres-
entation, where our mother bows in her thanksgiv-
ings to the Holy God who has helped her in her time
of need; and who has equally made birth, and life,
and death, and as equally vouchsafed safety in each
and all? What is this that presseth in---chiefest of
guests---at our marriages, in all the splendor of his
yellowest glow; and waiting, with his face shrouded,
with his pale lights and abounding in ghostly tapers
---though in the glory of the hope of heaven!---at
that last, solemn scene, where the very cause of the
sable royalties---black (imperial, then, alike to poor
and rich in the common Spirit-threshold upon
which we all stand)---is as the smallest, and very
often the least thought-of, of all the show? What,
to conclude, is this *Fire* which is so constantly
about us, and of which we think so little and know
so little, but which seems over-whelmingly much?
What is this wondrous, universal Element, or least
proveable Soul of the World, which hath been so
significantly, and yet so unsuspectedly, mythed,
universally, through the intelligent ages? What is
this Magic reflection which is glassed through
Time. We ask thinkers for an answer. But only
out of their meditations---only out of the impossibility of denial---do we hope to wring the

confession of the Divine Spirit that is in the Fire.

"Of course we mean not, in this Real Fire, *but a something of which the Real Fire is an Image. Being the imparticled spirit, in which everything is at one, as in which everything is possible. In this sense, real things* (in the World) *are the things only unreal. And unreal things* (out of the World) *are the only real.*

Through two baptismals must the Initiate pass. Through the baptism of both Fire and Water. The mysterious meaning of baptism by water is a symbolism prevailing through *all* faiths, Heathen and Christian. It is that of the earliest traditional or the Pythagorean Transmigration, not abjudged as by its vulgar reading, but as signifying the *onward dissolution*, into nothingness, of being, that is, of this being, through the farthest separated (save air, in which man always is, and therefore always is baptised) matter---water! This, therefore, is the only element for a rite. Holy water, and ablution, also signify the same although the church has lost the meaning. Thence, as from that next-loosest of matter---water, the only possible symbol for a rite. Man is delivered into the farther, supernatural, airy changes, where matter ceases---loosening utterly from above him. And, then, the Spirit of Fire, begins, taking up the matter-undulations. This is the freedom into the foundation, or inspiring Light;---the Nirvana of the Buddhists;---the God Flame of the Magi;---the Holy Spirit of the Christians;---the everything, out of this state, and the nothing in it, of *all* religions. Life---nay, all existence---being considered as a Purgatory of a severer or a more assuasive order.   And, therefore, being evil---or God's Shadow---for the very reason of its being Life---or consciousness at all.   All consciousness being defect---all the outside world being evil.

This is the Mystic meaning of that text in the Holy Testament where St. John declares: "I indeed baptize you with water unto repentance: but he that comes after me is mightier than I, whose shoes I am not worthy to bear: he shall baptize you with the *Holy Ghost, and with Fire.*"

Fire-Philosophy

—

The Foundation of all True Initiation and all Mystic and Occult Fraternities, as well as the Secret Doctrine and the Ancient Mysteries.

—

(CONCLUDED.)

—

Sacred Fire

—

"THE appearance of God to mortals seems always to have been in brightness and great glory, whether He was angry and in displeasure, or benign and kind. These appearances are often mentioned in Scriptures. When God appeared on Mount Sinai, it is said, "The Lord descended upon it in Fire" (Exodus xix. 18). And when Moses repeats the history of this to the children of Israel, he says: "The Lord spake unto you out of the midst of the Fire" (Deuteronomy iv. 12). So it was when the Angel of the Lord appeared to Moses in a flame of fire out of the midst of the bush: "The bush burned with Fire, and the bush was not consumed" (Exodus iii. 3). The appearance of the Angel of God's presence, or that Divine Person who re presented God, were always in brightness; or, in

8

other words, the Shechinah was always surrounded with glory.   This seems to have given occasion to those of old to imagine fire to be what God dwelt in.

"Whether it was that any fire proceeded from God, and burnt up the oblation in the first sacrifices, as some ingenious men have conjectured, we know not.   It is certain that in after ages this was the case.   We are sure that a fire from the Lord consumed upon the altar the burnt offering of Aaron (Leviticus ix. 24); and so it did the sacrifice of Gideon, "both the flesh and the unleavened cakes" (Judges vi. 21).   When David built an altar unto the Lord, and offered burnt offerings and peace-offerings, and called upon the Lord, He answered him from heaven by Fire, upon the altar of burnt offerings" (Chronicles xxi. 26).   The same thing happened at the dedication of Solomon's temple: "The Fire came down from heaven, and consumed the burnt offering and the sacrifices, and the glory of the Lord filled the house" (2 Chronicles vii. 1). And much about a hundred years afterwards, when Elijah made that extraordinary sacrifice in proof that Baal was no god, "The Fire of the Lord fell and consumed the burnt sacrifice, and the wood, and the stones, and the dust, and licked up the water that was in the trench" (1 Kings xviii. 38). And if we go back long before the times of Moses, as early as Abraham's days, we meet with an instance of the same sort: "It came to pass that when the sun went down, and it was dark, behold a smoking furnace and a burning lamp, that passed between these pieces" (Genesis xv. 17).

"The first appearance of God, then, being in glory—or, which is the same thing, in light or fire —and He showing His acceptance of sacrifices in so many instances by consuming them with fire, hence it was that the Eastern people, and particu-larly the Persians, fell into the worship of fire itself, or rather they conceived fire to be the symbol of God's presence, and they worshiped God in, or by, fire. From the Assyrians, or Chaldaeans, or Per-sians, this worship was propagated southward among the Egyptians, and westward among the Greeks; and by them it was brought into Italy. The Greeks were wont to meet together to worship their *Prytaneia,* and there they consulted for the public Good; and there was a constant fire kept up-on the altar, which was dignified by the name of Vesta by some. The fire itself was properly Vesta; and so Ovid:

"Nec te aliud Vestam, quam vivam intelligere flammam."

The *Prytaneia* were the *atria* of the temples, where-in a fire was kept that was never suffered to go out. On the change in architectural forms from the pyra-midal (or the horizontal) to the obeliscar (or the up-right, or vertical,) the flames were transferred from the altars, or cubes, to the summits of the typical uprights, or towers; or to the tops of the candles, such as we see them used now in Catholic worship, and which are called "tapers," from their tapering or pyramidal form, and which are supposed always to indicate the Divine presence of influence. This, through the symbolism that there is in the Living Light, which is the last exalted show of fluent or of

inflamed brilliant matter, passing off into the unknown and unseen world of celestial light (or Occult
Fire), to which all the forms of things tend, and in
which even idea itself passes from recognition as
meaning, and evolves—spring up, as all flame does,
to escape, and to WING away.

"Vesta, or the fire, was worshiped in circular
temples, which were the images, or the miniatures,
of the "temple" of the world, with its dome, or cope,
of stars.   It was in the ATRIA of the temples, and
in the presence of and before the above-mentioned
lights, and the forms of ceremonial worship were
always observed.   It is certain that Vesta was
worshiped at Troy; and Aeneas brought her into
Italy:

" manibus vittas, Vestamque potentem, AEternumque adytis
effert penetralibus Ignem.'—*AEneid*, ii. 298.

Numa settled an order of Virgin Priestesses,
whose business and care it was constantly to maintain the Holy Fire.   And long before Numa's day,
we find it not only customary, but honorable, among
the Albans to appoint the best-born virgins to be
Priestesses of Vesta, and to keep up the constant,
unextinguished fire.

It is from this that sprang the Catholic Vestals so
well known throughout all civilized nations.   This
worship was all purity in its beginning but like
many other pure Religions, it has been abused to
such an extent that the underlying principle is not
recognizable.   The foundation of Fire worship is
in God and no man can say that it is a heathen religion.

"When Virgil speaks (*AEbeid*, iv. 200) of Iarbas, in Africa, as building a hundred temples and a hundred altars, he says:

"vigilemque sacra verat Ingem, Excubian Divum aeternas,"—

that he had "concentrated a fire that never went out." And he calls these temples and these lights, or this fire, the *"Perpetual Watches,"* of *"Watch-Lights,"* or *proof of the presence, of the Gods.* By which expressions he means, *that the places and things were constantly protected and solemnized where such lights burned, and that the celestials, or angel-defenders, "camped," as it were, and were sure to be met with thickly, where these flames upon the altars, and these torches or lights about the temples, were studiously and incessantly maintained.*

There is a mighty truth in this and the Occultist or Mystic should profit by these things. It is his duty while in "practice" to have not only a small light burning but incense as well for where the light and incense is, the impure spirits or Elementals will not enter while it is undergoing the "drill" that leads towards to the Development. Again, "when you see the Light Listen to the Voice of the Light" has a great meaning. The Catholic Church has a mighty truth in its burning candles and mankind will learn the truth of this in the coming ages.

"Thus the custom seems to have been general from the earliest antiquity to maintain a constant fire, as conceiving the Gods present there. And this was not only the opinion of the inhabitants in Judaea, but it extended all over Persia, Greece, Italy, Egypt, and most other nations of the world.

8 I

Even Masonry of the present age will have no Initiation without its Lighted tapers. WHY?

"Porphyry imagined that the reason why the most ancient mortals kept up a constant, ever-burning fire in honor of the immortal Gods was because Fire was most like the Gods. He says that the ancients kept an unextinguished fire in their temples to the Gods because it was most like them. Fire was not like the Gods, but it was what they appeared in to mortals, And so the true God always appeared in brightness and glory; yet no one would say that brightness was most like the true God, but was most like the *Shechinah*, in which God appeared. And hence the custom arose of keeping up an unextinguished fire in the ancient temples.

"God, then, being wont to appear in Fire, and being conceived to dwell in Fire, the notion spread universally, and was universally admitted. First, then, it was not at all out of the way to think of engaging in friendship with God by the same means as they contracted friendship with one another. And since they to whom God appeared saw Him appear in Fire, and they acquainted other with such His appearances, He was conceived to dwell in Fire. By degrees, therefore, the world came to be over-curious in the fire that was constantly to be kept up, and in things to be sacrificed; and they proceeded from one step to another, till at length they filled up the measure of their aberrations, which were in reality instigated by their zeal, and by their intense desire to mitigate the displeasure of their divinities —for religion was much more intense as a feeling

in earlier days—by passing into dreadful ceremonies in regard to this fire, which they reverenced
as the last possible physical form of divinity; not
only in its grandeur and power, but also in its purity.   It arose from this view that human sacrifices
came to be offered to the deities in many parts of
the world, particularly in Phoenicia, and in the colonies derived from thence to Africa and other places.
In the intensity of their minds, children were sacrificed by their parents, as being the best and dear-
est oblations that could be made, and the strongest
arguments that nothing ought to be withheld from
God.   This was expiation for that sad result, the
consequence of the original curse, issuing from the
fatal curiosity concerning the bitter fruit of that
forbidden "Tree,"

"whose mortal taste Brought death into the world, and all
our woe, With loss of Eden,"

according to Milton.   That sense of shame in all
its forms lesser and greater, and with all the refer-
ences inseperably allied to propagation in all its
multitudinous cunning (so to speak), wherever the
condemned material tissues reach, puzzled the
thoughtful ancients.   This they considered the convicted "Adversary," or "Lucifer," "Lord of Light"
—that is, material light—"Eldest son of the Morning."   Morning, indeed! dawning with its beams
from behind that forbidden Tree of Knowledge of
good and Evil.   What is this shame, urged the philosophers, this reddening, however good and beautiful, and especially the ornament of the young and
of children, who are newest from the real, glowing

countenance of Deity, with the bloom of the first
angelic world scarcely yet fading from off their
cherub faces, gradually darkening and hardening
in the degradation and iniquity of being here as
presences in the world, although the most glorious
amidst the forms of flesh? What is this shame,
which is the characteristic singly of human creatures? All other creatures are sinless in this respect, and know not the feeling of that—correctly
looked at—strange thing which men call "shame,"
something which it is not right that the sun ever
should see, and therefore stirring the blood, and
reddening the face, and confusing the speech, and
causing man to hang down his head, and to hide
himself, as if guilty of something; even as our guilty first parents, having lost the unconsciousness of
their child-like, innocent first state—that of sinless
virginity—hid themselves in the umbrage of Para-
dise, all at once convicted to the certainty that they
must hide, because they were exposed in the face
of that original intention regarding them having
been broken.

"Suffer little children to come unto Me, and for-
bid them not, for of such is the kingdom of heaven."

"That is, the innocent children should come up
for salvation, who, though suffering under the mortal liability incurred by all flesh in that first sin
(and incident in the first fall, which has empoisoned
all nature), are yet free by the nature of *that* un-
grown possibility, and from their immature state.
They know not the shame of that condition adult,
and therefore they bear not the badge of men.

"The pyramidal or triangular form which Fire assumes in its ascent to heaven is in the monolithic typology used to signify the great generative power. We have only to look at Stonehenge, Ellora, the Babel-towers of Central America, the gigantic ruins scattered all over Tartary and India, to see how gloriously they symbolised the majesty of the Supreme.   To these upright, obelisks, or LITHOI, of the old world, including the *Bethel*, or Jacob's Pillar, or Pillow, raised in the plain of "Luz," we will add, as the commemorative or reminding shape of the Fire, the Pyramids of Egypt, the Millenarius, Gnomon, Mete-Stone, or Mark, called London-Stone," all Crosses raised at the junction of four roads, all Market-crosses, the Round-Towers of Ireland, and in all the changeful aspects of their genealogy, all spires and towers, in their grand hieroglyphic proclamation, all over the world.

Fire-Philosophy of the Persians

"As a great general principle, the Theosophists called the Soul a Fire, taken from the eternal ocean of Light.

"In regard to the supernatural—using the word in its widest sense—it may be said that "all the difficulty in admitting the strange things told us lies in the non-admission of an internal causal world *as absolutely* real: it is said, in *intellectually* admitting, because the influence of the arts proves that man's feelings always have admitted, and do still admit, this reality.

"The Platonic philosophy of Vision is, that it is the view of objects really existing in *interior* Light, which assume form, not according to arbitrary laws, but according to the state of Mind. This *interior* light, if we understand Plato, unites with exterior light in the eye, and is thus drawn into a sensual or imaginative activity; but when the outward light is separated, it reposes in its own serene atmosphere. It is, then, in this state of interior repose, that the usual class of religious, or what are called inspired, visions, occur. It is the *same* light of eternity so frequently alluded to in books that treat of mysterious subjects; the light revealed to Pimander, Zoroaster, and all the sages of the East, as the emanation of the Spiritual Sun. Bohmen writes of it as his *Divine Vision of Contemplation*, and Molinos in his *Spiritual Guide*,—whose work is the ground of Quietism: *Quietism being the foundation of the religion of the people called Friends or Quakers, as also of the other Mystic or meditative sects.* We enlarge from a very learned, candid, and instructive book upon the Occult Science.

"Regard Fire, then, with *other* eyes than with those soul-*less*, incurious ones, with which thou hast looked upon it as the most ordinary thing. Thou hast forgotten what it is—or rather thou hast *never* known. Chemists are silent about it; or, may we not say that it is too *loud* for them? Therefore shall they speak fearfully of it in whispers. Philosophers talk of it as anatomists discourse of the continents (or the parts) of the human body—as a piece of mechanism, wondrous though it be. Such the wheels of the clock, say they in their ingenious expounding of the "whys" and the "wherefores" (and the mechanics and the mathematics) of this mysterious thing, with a supernatural soul in it, called world. Such is the chain, such are the balances, such the larger and the smaller mechanical forces; such the "Time-blood," as it were, that is sent circulating through it; such is the striking, with an infinity of bells. It is made for man, this world, and it is greatly *like* him—that is, *mean*, they would add.

"Note the goings of the Fire, as he creepeth, serpentineth, riseth, slinketh, broadeneth. Note him reddening, glowing, whitening. Tremble at his face, dilating; at the meaning that is growing into it, to you. See that spark from the blacksmith's anvil!—struck, as an insect, out of a sky containing a whole cloud of such. Rare locusts, of which Pharaoh and the Cities of the Plain read of old the Secret! One, two, three sparks;—dozens come:—faster and faster the fiery squadrons follow, until, in a short while, a whole possible army of that hungry thing for battle, for food for it— Fire—glances up; but is soon warned in again!— lest acres should glow in the growing advance. Think that this thing is bound as in matter-chains. Think that He is outside of all things, and deep in the *inside* of *all* things; and that thou and thy world are only *the thing between:* and that outside and inside are both identical, couldst thou understand the supernatural truths! Reverence Fire (for its Meaning), and tremble at it; though in the Earth it

be chained, and the foot of the Archangel Michael
—like upon the Dragon—be upon it! Avert the
face from it, as the Magi turned, dreading, and (as
the symbol) before it bowed askance. So much for
this *Great* thing—Fire!

''Observe the multiform shapes of fire; the flame-
wreaths, the spires, the stars, the spots, the cas-
cades, and the mighty falls of it; where the roar,
when it grows high in Imperial masterdom, as that
of Niagara. Think what it can do, what it is.
Watch the trail of sparks, struck, as in that spouting arch, from the metal shoes of the trampling
horse. It is a letter of the great alphabet. The
familiar London streets, even, can give the
Persian's God: though in thy pleasures, and in
thy commerce-operations, thou so oft forgettest
thine *own* God. Whence liberated are those
sparks?...as stars, afar off, of a whole sky
of flame;...sparks, deep down in possibility, though
close to us;...great in their meaning, though small
in their show;...as distant single ships of whole
fiery fleets;...animate children ot, *in* thy human
conception, a dreadful but, in reality, a great world,
of which thou knowest nothing. They fall, foodless,
on the rejecting, barren, and (on the outside) the
coldest stone. But in each stone, fence flinty and
chilling as the outside is, *is a heart of fire*, to strike
at which is to bid gush forth the *waters*, as it were,
of every fire, like waters of the rock! Truly, out of
sparks can be displayed a whole acreage of fire-
works. Forests can be conceived of flame—palaces
of the fire; Grandest things—Soul-things—last
things—all things!

"Wonder no longer, then, if, rejected so long as an idolatry, the ancient Persians, and their Masters the Magi,—concluding that they saw "All" *in* this supernaturally magnificent element,—fell down and worshipped it; making of it the Visible *representation* of the *very truest;* but yet, in man's speculation, and in his philosophers,—nay, in his commonest reason,— impossible God: God being *everywhere*, and *in* us, indeed, *us*, in the God-lighted man; and impossible to be contemplated or known outside,—being *All!*

"Lights and flames, and the *torches*, as it were, of fire (all fire in this world, the last background on which all things are painted), may be considered as "lancets" of another world—the last world: circles, enclosed by the thick walls (which, however, *by the Fire* are kept from closing) of this world. As fire and brandishes, will the walls of this world wave, and, as it were, undulate from about it. In smoke and disruption, or combustion of matter, we wit-ness a phenomenon of the *burning* as of the edges of the matter-rings of this world, in which world *is* fire, like a spot; that dense and hard thing, mat-ter, holding it in. Oxygen, which is the finest of air, and is the means of the quickest burning out, or the supernatural (in this world) exhilaration of animal life, or extenuation of the Solid; and, above all, the heightening of the capacity of the Human, as being the quintessence of matter: this oxygen is the thing which feeds fire the most overwhelm-ingly. Nor would the specks and spots and stars of fire stop in this dense world-medium,—in this

tissue or sea of things,—could it farther and farther fasten upon and devour the solids: eating, as it
were, through them.   But as this thick world is a
thing the thickest, it presses out, thrusts, or gravi-
tates upon, and stifles, in its too great weight; and
conquers not only that livliest, subtlest, thinnest
element of the solids, the finest air, by whatever
chemical name—*Oxygen*, *Azote*, *Azone*, or what not—
it may be called; which, in fact, is merely the nom-
enclature of its *composition*, the naming of the in-
gredients which make the thing (but not the thing).
The denseness of the world not only conquers this,
we repeat; but, so to figure it, matter stamps upon,
effaces, and treads out fire: which, else, would burn
on, back, as in the beginning of things, or into *itself*,
—consuming, as in its great revenge of anything
being created *other than it*, all the mighty worlds
which, in Creation, were permitted out of it.   This
is the teaching of the ancient Fire-Philosophers
reestablished and restored, to the days of comprehension of them, in the conclusions of the Rosicrucians of later times), who claimed to have discovered
the Eternal Fire, or to have found out "God" in the
"Immortal Light."*

   "There are all grades or graduations of the den-
sity of matter; but it all coheres by the one law of
gravitation.   Now, this gravitation is mistaken for
a force of itself, when it is nothing *but the sympathy,
or the taking away of the supposed thing between two
other things.*   It is sympathy (or appetite) seeking

---

*See "Divine Alchemy" for the mystery of Fire—Sex.

its food, or as the closing together of two things.
It is not because one mass of matter is more ponderable or attractive than another (out of our senses,
and in reality), but that they are the same, with
different amounts of affection, and that like seeks
like, not recognizing or knowing that between.
Now, this thing which is, as it were, slipped between, and which we strike into show of itself, or
into fire—surprised and driven out of its ambush---
is Fire. It is as the letter by which matter spells
itself out---so to speak. Now, matter is only to be
finally forced asunder by heat; flame being the
bright, subtle something which comes last, and is
the expansion, fruit, crown or glory of heat: it is
the vivid and visible soul, essence, and spirit of heat
---the last evolvement before rending, and before
the forcible closing again of all the center-speeding
weights, or desires, of matter. Flame is the expanding out (or even *exploding*) flower to this growing thing, heat: it is at the bubble of it---the fruit
(to which before we have likened it), or seed, in the
outside Hand upon it. Given the super-natural
Flora, heat is as the gorgeous plant, and flame the
glorifying flower; and as growth is greater out of
the greater *matrix*, or matter of growing, so the
thicker the material of fire (as we may roughly figure it, though we hope we shall be understood), so
the stronger shall be the fire, and of necessity the
fiercer will it be perceived to be---result being according to power.

"Thus we get more of fire---that is, heat---out of
the hard things: there being more of the thing Fire
in them.

"But Fire disjoints, as it were, all the hinges of the house—laps out the coherence of it—sets ablaze the dense thing, matter—makes the dark metals run like waters of light—conjures the black devils out of the minerals, and, to our astonishment, shows them much libelled, blinding, angel-white! By Fire we can lay our hands upon the solids, Part them, powder them, melt them, fine them, drive them out to more and more delicate and impalpable texture—firing their invisible molecules, or imponderables, into clouds, into mist, into gas: out of seeing, into smelling; out of smelling into nothing—into real *nothing*---not even into the last blue sky. These are the potent operations of Fire---the crucible into which we cast all the worlds, and find them, in their last evolution, not even smoke. These are physical and scientific facts which there can be no gainsaying---which were seen and found out long ago, ages ago, in the reveries first, and then in the practice, of the great Magnetists (Rosicrucians), and those who were called the Fire-Philosophers, of whom we have spoken before.

"What is that mysterious and inscrutable operation, the striking fire from flint? Familiar as it is, who remarks it? Where, in that hardest, closest pressing together of matter---where the granulation compresses, shining even in its hardness, into the solidest *Laminae* of cold, darkest, blue, and streaky, core-like, agate-resembling white---lie the seeds of fire, spiritual flame-seeds to the so stony fruit? In what folds of the flint, in the block of it —in what invisible recess—speckled and spotted, in what tissue—crouch the fire-sparks?—to issue, in showers, on the stroke of iron—on the so sudden clattering (as of the crowbars of man) on its stony doors: Stone craving the thing Fire, unseen, as its sepulchre; Stroke warning the magical thing forth. Whence comes that trail of fire from the cold bosom of the hard, secret, unexploding flint?—Children as from what hard, rocky breast; yet hiding its so sacred, sudden fire-birth!   Who—and what science-philosopher---can explain this wondrous darting forth of the hidden something, which he shall try in vain to arrest, but which, like a spirit, escapes him?   If we ask what fire is, of the men of science, they are at fault.   They will tell us that it is a *phenomenon*, that their vocabularies can give no further account of it.   They will explain to us that all can be said of it is, that it is a last affection of matter, to the results of what (in the world of man) they can only testify, but of whose coming and of whose going—of the place from which it comes, and the whereabouts of which it goeth---they are entirely ignorant,---and would give a world to know.

"The foregoing---however feebly expressed---are the views of the famous Rosicrucians* respecting the nature of this supposed familiar, but yet puzzling, thing---Fire.   We will proceed to some of their further Mystic reveries.

---

* For the *real* Mystery of the Fire Philosophy of the *true* Rosicrucians, see "Divine Alchemy."

9

Ideas of the Rosicrucians as to the Character of Fire

"Spark surrenders out of the world, when it disappears to us, in the universal ocean of Invisible Fire. That is its disappearance. It quits us in the supposed light, but *to it* really darkness—as fire-born, the last level of all—to reappear in the true light, which is *to us* darkness. This is hard to understand. But, as the real is the direct contrary of the apparent, so that which shows as light to us is darkness in the supernatural; and that which is light to the supernatural is darkness to us: matter being darkness, and Soul light. For we know that light is material, and, being material, it must be dark. For the Spirit of God is not material, and therefore, not being material, it cannot be light to us, and therefore darkness to God. Just as (until discovered otherwise) the world it is that is at rest, and the sun and the heavenly bodies in daily motion —instead of the very reverse being the fact. This is the belief of the oldest Theosophists, the founders of magical knowledge in the East, and the discoverers of the Gods, also the doctrine of the fire-Philosophers, and of the Rosicrucians who taught that all knowable things (both of the Soul and of the body) were evolved out of Fire, and finally resolvable into it; and that Fire was the last and only-to-be-known God: as that all things were capable of being searched down into it, and all things were capable of being thought up to it. Fire, they found, when, as it were, they took this world, solid, to pieces (and also, as metaphysicians, distributed and divided the mind of man, seeking for that invisible God-thing, coherence of ideas)---fire, these thinkers found, in their supernatural light of mind, to be the latent, nameless matter started out of the tissues-- certainly out of the body, presumably out of the mind---with groan, disturbance, hard motion, and *flash* (when forced to sight of it), instantly disappearing, and relapsing, and hiding its Godhood in the closing-violently-again solid matter---as into the forcefully resuming mind. Matter, the agent whose remonstrance at disturbance out of its Rest was, in the winds, murmur, noise, cries, as it were, of air; in the waters, rolling and roaring; in the piled floors of the sky, and their furniture, clouds, circumvolence, contest, and war, and thunders (defiant to nature, but groans to God), and intolerable lightning-rendings, matter tearing as a garment, to close supernaturally together again, as the Solid, fettered and chained---devil-bound---in the Hand upon it, "To Be!"   In this sense, all noise (as the rousing or conjuration of matter by the outside forces) is the agony of its penance.   All motion is pain, all activity punishment; and Fire *is the* secret, lowest---that is, foundation-spread---thing, the ultimate of all things, which is disclosed when the clouds of things roll, for an instant, off it,---as the blue sky shows, in its fragments, like turquoises, when the canopy of clouds is wind-torn, speck-like from off it.   Fire is that floor over which the coats or layers, or the spun kingdoms of matter, or of the subsidences of the past periods of time (which is built up of objects), are laid; tissues woven over a gulf of it: in one of which last, We Are.   To which Fire we only become sensible when we start it by blows or force, in the rending up of atoms, and in the blasting out of them that which holds them, which then, as Secret Spirit, springs compelled to sight, and as instantly flies, except to the immortal eyes, which receives it (in the supernatural) on the other side.

"The Fire-Philosophers maintained that we transcend everything into Fire, and that we lose it there in the flash, the escape of fire being as the door through which everything disappears to the other side.   In their very peculiar speculations, and in this stupendous and supernatural view of the universe, where we think that fire is the exception, and is, as it were, *spotted over the world* (in reality, to go out *when it goes out*), they held that the direct contrary was the truth, and that we, and all things, were *spotted upon fire;* and that we conquer patches only of fire when we put it out, or win torches out of the *great flame*, when we enkindle fire,—which is our master in the truth, making itself, in our beliefs (in our human needs), the slave.   Thus fire, when it is put out, only goes into the underworld, and the matter-flags close over it like a grave-stone.

"When we witness Fire, we are as if peering only through a door into another world.   Into this, all the (consumed into microscopical smallness) things of this world, the compressed and concentrate matter-heaps of defunct tides of Being and Time, are in combustion rushing: kingdoms of the floors of the things passed through—up to this moment held in suspense in the invisible inner worlds. All roars through the hollow. All this is mastered in the operations of this Fire, and that is rushing through the hollow made by it in the partition-world of the Knowable—across, and out on the other side, into the Unknowable—seeks, in the Fire, its last and most perfect evolution into *absolute nothing*,—as a bound prisoner urges to his feet, in his chains, and shrieks for freedom when he is smitten. In Fire, we witness a grand phenomenon of the subsidiary (or further, and under, and inner, and multiplied) birth and death, and the supernatural transit of microscopic worlds, passing from the human sense-worlds to other levels and into newer fields. Then it is that the Last Spirit, of which they are composed, is playing before us; and playing, and playing, into last extinction, out of its rings of this-side matter: all which matter, in its various stages of thickening, is as the flux of the Supernatural Fire, or inside God.

"It will appear no wonder now, if the above abstractions be caught by the Thinker, how it was that the early people (and the founders of Fire-Worship) considered that they saw God, standing face to face with Him—that is, with all that, in their innermost possibility of thought, they could find as God—in Fire. Which Fire is *not* our vulgar, gross fire; neither is it the purest material fire, which has something of the base, bright lights of the world still about it—brightest though they be in the matter which makes them the *Lightest* to the material sight; but it is an occult, mysterious, or *inner*—not even magnetic, but a supernatural—Fire: a real. sensible, and the only possible Mind, or God, as containing all things, and as the soul of all things; into whose inexpressible intense, and all-devouring and divine, though fiery, gulf, all the worlds in succession, like ripe fruit to the ground, and all things, fall,—back into whose arms of Immortal Light: on the other side, as again receiving them, all things, thrown off as the smoke off light, again fall!

"At the shortest, then, the theory of the Magi may be summed up thus. When, as we think, fire is spotted over all the world, as we have said, it is we who make the mistake, necessitated in our man's nature, and we are that which is spotted over it;— just as, while we think we move, we are moved; and we conclude the senses in us, while we are in the senses: everything—out of the world---being the very opposite of that which we take it. The views of these mighty thinkers amounted to the suppression of human reason, and the institution of Magic, or God-head, as all. It will be seen at once that this knowledge was possible but for the very few. It is only fit for men when they seek to pass out of the world, and to approach---the nearest according to their natures---God.

"The hollow world in which that essence of things, called Fire, plays, in its escape, in violent agitation ---to us, combustion,---is deep down inside of us:[*] that is, deep-sunk inside of the time-stages of which

[*] See "Divine Alchemy."

rings of being (subsidences of spirit) we are, in the flesh,---that is, in the human show of things,---in the *outer*. It is exceedingly difficult. through language, to make this idea intelligible; but it is the real Mystic dogma of the ancient Guebres, or the Fire-Believers, the successors of the Buddhists, or, more properly, Bhuddists.

"What is explosion? It is the lancing into the layers of worlds, whereinto we force, through turning the edges out and driving through; in surprisal of the reluctant, lazy, and secret nature, exposing the hidden, magically microscopical stores of things, passing inwards out of the accumulated rings of worlds, out of the (within) supernaturally buried wealth, rolled in, of the past, in the procession of Being. What is smoke but the disrupted vapor-world to the started soul-fire? The truth is, say the Fire-Philosophers, in the rousing of fire we suddenly come upon Nature, and start her violently out of her ambush of things, evoking her secretest and immortal face to us. Therefore is this knowledge not to be known generally to man; and it is to be assumed at the safest in the disbelief of it: that disbelief being as the magic casket in which it is locked. The keys are only for the Gods, or for godlike spirits.

"We imagine that it will be said that it is impossible that any religionists could have seriously entertained such extraordinary doctrines; but, incredible as it may seem,—because it requires much preparation to *understand them*,—it is certainly true, that it is only in this manner the ideas of the Di-

vinity of Fire, which we know once prevailed largely, can be made intelligible,—we mean to the philosopher, who knows how properly to value the ancient Thinkers, who were as giants in the earth.

"Obelisks, spires, minarets, tall towers, upright
stones (Menhits), monumental crosses, and architectural perpendiculars of every description, and,
generally speaking, all erections conspicuous for
height and slimness, were representatives of the
sworded, or of the pyramidal Fire. They bespoke,
wherever found, and in whatever age, the idea of
the First Principle, or *the male generation Emblem.**

"Having given, as we hope, some new views of
the doctrine of Universal Fire, and shown that
there has been error in imagining that the Persians
and the Ancient Fire-Worshippers were idolaters
simply of fire, inasmuch as, in bowing down before
it, they only regarded Fire *as a Symbol, or Visible
Sign*, or thing placed as standing *for the* Deity,—
having, in our preceding lines, disposed the mind
of the reader to consider as a matter of solemnity,
and of much greater general significance, this
strange fact of Fire-Worship, and endeavored to
show it as a portentous, first, all-embracing as all-
genuine principle,—we will proceed to exemplify
the wide-spread roots of the Fire-Faith. In fact,
we seem to recognize it everywhere.

"Instead of, in their superstition—making of fire
their God, they obtained Him—that is, all that we
can realize of Him; by which we mean, all that the

---

*See both "Divine Alchemy," and "Ancient Mystic Oriental Masonry."

human reason can find of the Last Principle—out
of it.   Already in their thoughts, had the Magi exhausted all possible theologies; already had they,
in their great wisdom, searched through physics—
their power to this end being much greater than
that of the modern faith-teachers and doctors; already, in their reveries, in their observations (deep
with their deep souls) upon the nature of themselves, and of the microcosm of a world in which
they found themselves, had the Magi transcended.
They had arrived at a new world in their speculations and deductions upon facts, upon all the things
behind which (to men) make these facts.   Already,
in their determined climbing into the heights of
thought, and these Titans of mind achieved, past
the cosmical, through the shadowy borders of Real
and Unreal, into Magic.

"Passing through the mind-worlds, and coming
out, as we may figure it, *at the other side*, penetrating into the secrets of things, they evaporated all
Powers, and resolved them finally into the Last
Fire.   Beyond this, they found nothing; as into
this they resolved all things.   And then, on the
Throne of the Visible, they placed this—in the
world Invisible—Fire: the sense thing to be worshipped *in the senses*, as the last thing of them, and
the king of them,—that is, that which we know as
the phenomenon, Burning Fire,—the Spiritual Fire
being inpalpable, as having the visible only for its
shadow; the Ghostly Fire not being even to be
thought upon; thought being its medium of apprehension when itself had slipped; the waves of ap-

prehension of it only flowing back when it—being intuition—had vanished. We only know that a thought is in us when the thought is off the object and in us: another thought being, at that simultaneous instant, in the object, to be taken up by us only when the first has gone out of us, and so on; but not *before* to be taken up by us,—that thought being *all of us*, and a deceptive and unreal thing to pass at all to us through the reason, and there being no resemblance between it and its original; the true thing being "Inspiration," or "God in us," excluding all matter or *reason*, which is only built up of matter. It is most difficult to frame language in regard to those things. Reason can only inmake God; He is only possible in His own development, or in His sieging of us, and "in possession." Thus Paracelsus and his disciples declare the Human Reason become our master, that is, in its perfection, ---but not use as our servant,---transforms, as it were into the Devil, and exercises *his* office in leading us away *from* the throne of Spiritual Light---over, and, in the world, seeming *better;* in his false and deluding World-Light, or Matter-Light, really showing himself God. This view of the Human Reason, intellectually trusted, transforming into the Angel of Darkness, and effacing God out of the world, is borne out by a thousand *Texts of Scripture.* It is equally in the beliefs and in the traditions of all nations and of all times, as we shall by and by show. Real Light *is* God's Shadow, or the soul of matter; the one is the very brighter, as the other is the very blacker. *Thus, the worshippers of the Sun,*

*or Light, or Fire,—otherwise they would have wor-
shipped the Devil, he being all conceivable Light: but
rather they adored the Unknown Great God, in the last
image that was possible to man of anything*—the Fire.

And they chose that as His shadow, as the very
opposite of that which He really was: honouring the
Master through His Servant; bowing before the
manifestation, Eldest of Time, for the Timeless;
paying homage to the spirit of the Devil-World, or
rather to Beginning and End, on which was the
foot of *ALL*, that the All, or the *LAST*, might be
worshipped; propitiating the Evil Principle in its
finite shows, because (as they that alone a world
could be made, whose making is alone Comparison)
it was permitted as a means of God, and therefore
the operation of God Downwards, as part of Him,
though Upwards dissipating as before Him,—before *HIM* in whose presence Evil, or Comparison,
or Difference, or Time, or Space, or anything,
should be Impossible: real God being not to be
thought upon.

"But it was not only in the quickening Spirit of
Divinity that these teachings could be seen. Otherwise than in faith, we can hope that they shall now
—in our weak attempts to explain them—be gathered as not contradictory, and merely intellectual,
and seen as vital and absolute. They need the elevation of the mind in the sense of "Inspiration,"
and not the quickening and *sharpening* of the Intellect, as seeking wings—devil-pinions—wherewith
to sail into the region only of its own laws, where,
of course, it will not find God. Then step in the

mathematics, then the senses, then the reason,---
then the very perfection of matter-work, or this
world's work, sets in,---engines of which the Sa-
tanic Powers shall realize the work. The evil Spirit conjures, as even by holy command, the trans-
lucent sky. The Archangelic, clear, child-like
rendering-up in intuitive belief,---intense in its own
sun,---is *Faith*. Lucifer fills the scope of belief with
imitative, dazzling clouds, and built splendours.
With these temptations it is sought to dissuade,
sought to rival, sought to put out Saints' sight---
sought even to surpass in seeming a farther and
truer, because a more solid and a more sensible,
glory. The apostate, real born Lucifer, is so named
as the intensest Spirit of Light, because he is of the
things that perish, and of the things that to Mind---
because they are all of Matter---have the most of
glory! Thus is one of the names of the Devil, the
very eldest-born and brightest Star of Light, that
of the very morning and beginning of all things---
the clearest, brightest, purest, as being soul-like,
of Nature; but only of Nature. Real Law, or Nature, is the Devil; real Reason is the Devil.

"Now we shall find, with a little patience, that
this transcendental, beyond-limit-or-knowledge ancient belief of the Fire-God is to be laid hand upon---
as, in a manner, we shall say---in all the stories (and
they, indeed, *are* all) where belief has grown,---yea,
as a thing with the trees and plants, as out of the
very ground,---in all the countries and continents---
and in both worlds. And out of this great fact of
its universal dissipation, as a matter of history the

most innate and coexistent, shall we not assume
this fire-doctrine as being of truth?---as a thing
really, fundamentally, and vitally true?   As in the
East, so in the West; as in the old time, so in the
new; as in the pre-Adamite and post-diluvian worlds,
so in the modern and latter-day world; surviving
through the ages, buried in the foundations of empires, locked in the rocks, hoarded in legends,
maintained in monuments, preserved in beliefs,
suggested in traditions, borne amidst the roads of
the multitude in emblems, gathered up---as the recurring, unremarked, supernaturally coruscant,
and yet secret, evading, encrusted, and dishonored
jewel---in rites, spoken (to those capable of the comprehension) in the field of hieroglyphics, dimly
glowing up to a fitful suspicion of it in the sacred
rites of all peoples; figured forth in the religions,
symbolized in a hundred ways: attested, prenoted,
bodied forth in occult body, as far as body can;---
in fine, in multitudinous fashions and forms forcibly soliciting the sharpness of sight directed to its
discovery, and spelt over a floor as underplacing all
things, we recognize, we spy, we descry, and we
may, lastly *admit* the mysterious sacredness of
Fire.   For why should we not admit it?

Monuments Raised to Fire-Worship in all Countries

"We think that we shall be able fully, in our suc-
ceeding pages, to place beyond contradiction an
extraordinary discovery.   It is that the whole

round of disputed emblems which so puzzle antiquaries, and which are found in all countries, point
to the belief in Fire as the First Principle. We
seek to show that the Fire-Worship was the very
earliest, from the immemorial times,---that it was
the foundation religion,---that the attestation to it
is preserved in monuments scattered all over the
globe,---that the rites and usages of all creeds, down
even to *our own day*, and in every-day use about us,
bear reference to it,---that problems and puzzles in
religion, which cannot be otherwise explained,
stand clear and evident when regarded in this new
light,---that in all the Christian varieties of belief---
as truly as in Bhuddism, in Mohammedanism, in
Heathenism of all kinds, whether eastern, or western, or northern, or southern---this "Mystery of
Fire" stands ever general, recurring, and conspicuous,--and that in being so, beyond all measure,
old, and so, beyond all modern, or any idea of it,
general,---as universal, in fact, as man himself, and
the thoughts of man,---and as being that beyond
which, in science and in natural philosophy, we cannot further go,---it must carry truth with it, however difficult to comprehend, and however unsuspected: that is; as really being the manifestation
and Spirit of God, and—to the confounding and
annihilation of Atheism—Revelation.

"Affirmatively we shall now, therefore, offer to
the attention of the reader the universal scattering
of the Fire-Monuments, taking up at the outset
certain positions about them.

"Narrowly considered, it will be found that all re-

ligions transcend up into this spiritual Fire-Floor,
on which, to speak metaphysically, the phases of
Time were laid.   Material Fire, which is the brighter as the matter which constitutes it is the blacker,
is the shadow (so to express, or to speak, necessarily with "words," which have no meaning in the
spirit) of the "Spirit-Light," which invests itself
in it as the mask in which alone it can be possible.
Thus, material light being the very opposite of
God, the Egyptians—who were undoubtedly acquainted with the Fire-Revelation—could not represent God as light.   They therefore expressed their
Idea of Deity by Darkness.   Their chief adoration
was paid to *darkness*.   They bodied the Eternal forth
under Darkness.

"Stones were set up by the Patriarchs: the Bible records them.   In India, the first objects of
worship were Monoliths.   In the two peninsulas
of India, in Ceylon, in Persia, in the Holy Land, in
Phoenicia, in Saramathia, in Scythia, everywhere
where worship was attempted (and in what place
where man exists is it not?), everywhere where
worship was practiced) and where, out of fear, did
not, first, come the Gods, and then their propitia-
tion?)—in all the countries, we repeat, as the earliest of man's work, we recognize this sublime, mys-
teriously speaking, ever-recurring monolith, mark-
ing up the tradition of the supernaturally real, and
only real, Fire-dogma.   Buried so far down in time,
the suspicion assents that there *must* somehow be
truth in the foundation; not fanciful, legendary,
philosophical creed-truth, unexplainable (and only

to be admitted without question) truth: but truth, however mysterious and aweing, yet cogent, and not to be of philosophy (that is, illumination) denied.

"The death and decent of Balder into the Hell of the Scandinavians may be supposed to be the purgatory of the Human Unit (or the God-illuminate), from the Light (through the God-dark phases of being), back into its native Light. Balder was the Scandinavian Sun-God, and the same as the Egyptian Osiris, the Greek Hercules, Bacchus, and Phœbus, or Apollo, the Indian Krishna, the Persian Mithras, the Aten of the Empires of Insular Asia; or, even of the Sidonians, the Athyr or Ashtaroth. The presence of all these divinities—indeed, of *all* Gods—were of the semblance of Fire; and we recognize, as it were, the mark of the foot of them, or of the Impersonated Fire, in the countless uprights, left, as memorials, in the great ebb of the ages (as waves) to nations in the later divisions of that great roll of periods called Time: yet to totally unguessing of the preternatural mystery—seeming the key of all belief, and the reading of all wonders—which they speak.

"It is to be noted that all the above religions— all the Creeds of Fire—were exceedingly similar in their nature; that they all fortified by rites, and fenced around with ceremonies; and that, associated as they were with mysteries and initiations, the disciple was led through the knowledge of them in stages, as his powers augmented and his eyes saw, until, towards the last grades (as if he himself grew capable and illuminate), the door was closed upon all after-pressing and unrecognized inquirers, and the Admitted One was himself lost sight of.

"There was a great wave to the westward of all knowledge, all cultivation of the arts, all tradition, all intellect, all civilization, all religious belief. The world was peopled westward. There seems some secret, divine impress upon the world's destinies — and, indeed, ingrained in cosmical matter — in these matters. All faiths seem to have diverged out, the narrower or the wider, as rays from the great central Sun of this tradition of the Fire-Original. It would seem that Noah, who is suspected to be the Fo, Foh, or Fohi, of the Chinese, carried it into the farthest Cathay of the middle ages. What is the Chinese Tien, or Earliest Fire? The pagodas of the Chinese (which name, *Pagoda*, was borrowed from the Indian; from which country of India, indeed, probably came into China its worship, and its Bhuddist doctrine of the exhaustion back into the divine light, or unparticled nothingness, of all the stages of being or of Evil),—the Chinese pagodas, we repeat, are nothing but innumerable gilt and belled fanciful repetitions of the primeval monolith. The fire, or light, is still worshipped in the Chinese temples; it has not been perceived that, in the very form of the Chinese Pagodas, the fundamental article of the Chinese religion — transmigration, through stages of being, out into nothingness of this world — has been architecturally emblemed in the diminishing stories, carried upwards, and fining away into the series of unaccountable discs struck through a vertical rod, until all culminates,

10

and—as it were, to speak heraldically of it—the
last *achievement* is blazoned in the gilded ball, which
means the final, or Bhuddist, glorifying absorption.
Buildings have always telegraphed the *Insignia* of
the mythologies; and, in China, the fantastic speaks
the sublime. We recognize the same embodied
Mythos in all architectural spiring or artistic dim-
inution, whether tapering to the globe or exaltation
of the Egyptian *Uraeus*, or the disc, or the Sidonian
crescent, or the lunar horns, or the *Acroterium* of
the Greek temple, or the pediment of the classic
Pronaos itself (crowning, how grandly and suggest-
ively, at solemn dawn, or in the "spirit-lusyres"
of the dimming and still more than dawn, solemn
twilight, the top of some mountain, an ancient of
the days). Here, besetting us at every turn, meet
we the same mystic emblem; again, in the crescent
of the Mohammedan fanes, surmounting even the
Latin, and therefore the once Christian St. Sophia.
Last, and not least, the countless "churches" rise,
in the Latter-Day Dispensation, sublimely to the
universal signal, in the glorifying, or top, or crowning Cross: last of the Revelation!

"In the fire-towers of the Sikls, in the dome-
covered and many-storied spires of the Hindoos, in
the vertically turreted and longitudinally massed
temples of the Bhudds, of all the classes and of all
the sects, in the religious building of the Cingalese,
in the upright flame-fanes of the Parsees, in the
original of the *Campaniles* of the Italians, in the
tower of St. Mark at venice, in the flame-shaped or
pyramidal (*Pyr* is the Greek for Fire) architecture

of the Egyptians (which is the parent of all that is called architecture), we see the recurring symbol. All the minarets that, in the eastern sunshine, glisten through the Land of the Moslem; indeed, his two-horned crescent, equally with the moon, or disc, or two-pointed globe of the Sidonian Ashtaroth (after whose forbidden worship Solomon, the wisest of mankind, in his defection from the God of his fathers, evilly thirsted); also, the mystic *discus*, or "round," of the Egyptians, so continually repeated; and set, as it were, as the forehead-mark upon all the temples of the land of soothsayers and sorcerers,—this Egypt so profound in its philosophies, in its wisdom, in its magic-seeing, and in its religion, raising out of the black Abyss a God to shadow it, all the minarets of the Mohammedan, we say, together with all the other symbols of moon or disc, or wings, or of horns (equally with the shadowy and preternatural beings in all mythologies and in all theologies, to which these adjuncts or *Insignia* are referred, and which are symbolized by them),—all these monuments, or bodied meanings, testify to the Deification of Fire.

"What may mean that "Tower of Babel" and its impious raising, when it sought, even past and over the clouds, to imply a daring sign? What portent was that betrayal of a knowledge not for man,— that surmise forbidden save in infinite humility, and in the whispered impartment of the further and seemingly more impossible, and still more greatly mystical, meanings? In utter abnegation of self alone shall the mystery of fire be conceived.

Of what was this Tower Belus, or the Fire, to be the monument? When it soared, as a *Pharos*, on the rock of the traditionary ages, to defy time in its commitment, to "form" of the unpronounceable secret,—stage on stage and story on story, though it climbed the clouds, and on its top should shine the ever-burning Fire,—first idol in the world, "dark save with neglected stars,"—what was the Tower of Babel but a gigantic monolith? Perhaps to record and to perpetuate this ground-fire of all; to be worshipped, in idol, in its visible form, when it should be alone taken as the invisible *thought:* fire to be waited for (spirit possession), not waited on (idolatry.) Therefore was the speech confounded, that the thing should not be; therefore, under the myth of climbing into heaven by the means of it, was the first colossal monolithic temple (in which the early dwellers upon the earth sought to enshrine the Fire) laid prostrate in the thunder of the Great God. And the languages were confounded from that day,—speech was made babble—thence its name,—that the secret should remain a secret. It was to be only darkly hinted, and to be fitfully disclosed, like a false-showing light, in the theosophic glimmer, amidst the world's knowledge-lights. It was to reappear, like a spirit, to the "initiate," in the glimpse of reverie, in the snatches of sight, in the profoundest wisdom, through the studies of all ages.

"We find, in the religious administration of the ancient world, the most abundant proofs of the secret fire-tradition. Sehweigger shows, in his

"*Introduction into Mythology*" (pp. 132, 228), that the Phoenician Cabiri and the Greek Dioscuir, the Curetes, Corybantes, Telchini, were originally of the same nature, and are only different in trifling particulars. All these symbols represent electric and magnetic phenomena, and that under the ancient name of twin-fires, hermaphrodite fire. The Diescuri is a phrase equivalent to the Sons of Heaven: if, as Herodotus asserts, "Zeus originally represented the whole circle of Heaven."

"From India into Egypt was imported this Spiritual Fire-Belief. We recognize, again, its never-failing structure-signal. Rightly regarded the great Pyramids are nothing but the world-enduring architectural attestation, following (in the pyramidal) the well-known leading law of Egypt's templar piling mound-like, spiry—of the Universal Flame-Faith. Place a light upon the summit, star-like upon the sky, and a prodigious altar the mighty Pyramid then becomes. In this tribute to the world-filling faith, burneth expressed devotion to (radiateth acknowledgement of) the immortal magic religion. There is little doubt that as token and emblem of Fire-worship, as indicative of the adoration of the *real*, accepted Deity, these Pyramids were raised.* The idea that they were burial places of the Egyptian monarchs is untenable when submitted to the weighing of meanings, and when it comes side by side with this better fire-explanation.

See "Ancient Mystic Oriental Masonry" regarding the use the Fire Monuments were put to.

Cannot we accept these Pyramids as the vast altars on whose top should burn the *flame*—flame commemorative, as it were, to all the world, Cannot we see in these piles, literally and really Transcendental in origin, the Egyptian reproduction, and a hieroglyphical signalling on, of special truth, eldest of time? Do we not recognize in the Pyramid the repetition of the first monolith?—all the uprights constituting the grand attesting pillar to the supernatural traditions to a Fire-Forn World?

The ever-recurring Globe with Wings, so frequent in the sculptures of the Egyptians, witness to the Electric Principle. It embodies the transmigration of the Indians, reproduced by Pythagoras. Pythagoras resided for a long period in Egypt, and acquired from the priests the philosophic "transition"—knowledge, which was afterwards doctrine. The globe, disc, or circle of the Phoenician Astarte, the crescent of Minerva, the horns of the Egyptian Ammon, the deifying of the ox,—all have the same meaning. We trace, among the Hebrews, the token of the identical mystery in the horns of Moses, distinct in the sublime statue by Michael Angelo in the Vatican; as also in the horns of the Levitical altar: indeed, the use of the "double Hieroglyph" in continental ways. The *volutes* of the Ionic column, the twin stars of Castor and Pollux, nay, generally, the employment of the double emblem all the world over, in ancient or in modern times, whether displayed as points, or *radii*, or wings on the helmets of those barbarian chiefs who made war upon Rome, Attila or Genséric, or

broadly shown upon the head-piece of the Frankish
Clovis; whether emblemed in the rude and, as it
were, savagely, mystic horns of the Asiatic Idols,
or reproduced in the horns of the Runic Hammerer
(or Destroyer), or those of the Gothic Mars, or of
the modern Devil—All this double-spreading from
a common point (or this figure of *HORNS*) speaks
the same story.

"The Colossus of Rhodes was a monolith, in the
human form, dedicated to the Sun, or the Fire.
The Pharos of Alexandria was a fire-monument.
Heliopolis, or the City of the Sun, in Lower Egypt
(as the name signifies), contained a temple, wherein,
combined with all the dark superstitions of the
Egyptians, the flame-secret was preserved. In
most jealous secrecy was the tradition guarded,
and the symbol alone was presented to the world.
Of the Pyramids, as prodigious Fire-Monuments,
we have before spoken. Magnificent as the principal Pyramid still is, it is stated by an ancient his-
torian that it originally formed, at the base, "a
square of eight hundred feet, and that it was eight
hundred feet high." Another informs that "three
hundred and sixty-six thousand men were employed
twenty years in its erection." Its height is now
supposed to be six hundred feet. Have historians
and antiquaries carefully weighed the fact (even in
the *name* of the Pyramids), that *Pyr*, or *Pur*, in the
Greek, means *Fire?* We would argue that that
object, in the Great Pyramid, which has been mistaken for a tomb (and which is, moreover, rather
fashioned like an altar, smooth and plain, without

any carved work), is, in reality, the vase, urn, or
depository, of the sacred, ever-burning *FIRE*: of the
existence which ever-living, inextinguishable fire,
to be found at some period of the world's history,
there is abundant tradition.   This view is fortified
by the statements of Diodorus, who writes that
"Cheops, or Chemis, who founded the principal
Pyramid, and Chephren, or Cepherenus, who built
the next to it, were neither buried here, but that
they were deposited elsewhere.

"It is evident from their hieroglyphics that the
Egyptians were acquainted with the wonders of
magnetism. By means of it (and by the secret
power which lie in the *hyper-sensual*, "heaped floors'
of it), out of the every-day senses, the Egyptians
struck together, as it were, a bridge, across which
they paraded into the supernatural:, the Magic portals receiving them as on the other and *armed* side
of a drawbridge, shaking in its thunders in its raising (or in its lowering), as out of flesh. Athwart
this, in TRANCES, swept the Adepts, leaving their
mortality behind them. *All*, and their earth-sur-
roundings, to be resumed at their reissue upon the
plains of life, when down in their humanity again.

"In the cities of the ancient world, the Palladium,
or Protesting Talisman (invariably set up in the
chief square of place), was—there is but little doubt
—the reiteration of the very earliest monolith. All
the obelisks,—each often a single stone, of prodigious weight,—all the singular, solitary, wonderful
pillars and monuments of Egypt, as of other lands,
are, as it were, only tombstones of the Fire! All

testify to the great, so darkly hinted secret. In
Troy was the image of Pallas, the myth of knowledge, of the world, of manifestation, of the Fire,
Soul. In Athens was Pallas-Athene, or Minerva. In the Greek cities, the form of the deity
changed variously to Bacchus, to Hercules, to Phœ-
bus-Apollo; to the tri-formed Minerva, Dian, and
Hecate; to the dusky Ceres, or the darker Cybele,
In the wilds of Sarmathia, in the wastes of Northern Asia, the luminous rays descended from heaven,
and, animating the Lama, or "Light-Born," spoke
the same story. The flames of the Greeks, the
towers of the Phœnicians, the emblems of the Pe-
lasgi; the story of Prometheus, and the myth of his
stealing the fire from Heaven, wherewith to ani-
mate the man (or enSoul the visible world); the
forges of the Cyclops, and the monuments of Sicily;
the mysteries of the Etrurians: the rites of the
Carthaginians; the torches borne, in all priestly
demonstrative processions, at all times, in all countries; the Vestal Fires of the Romans, the very
word *Flamen*, as indicative of the office of the officiating sacerdote; the hidden fires of the ancient
Persians, and the grimmer (at least in name) Guebres; the whole Mystic meaning of flames on altars,
of the ever-burning tomb-lights of the earlier peoples, whether in the classic or in the barbarian
lands,—everything of this kind was intended to signify the deified Fire. Fires are lighted in the funeral ceremonies of the Hindoos and of the Moham-
medans, even to this day, though the body be com-
mited whole to earth. Wherefore fire, then? Cre-

mation and urn-burial, or the burning of the dead
—practiced in all ages—imply a profounder meaning than is generally supposed. They point to the
transmigration of Pythagoras, or to the purgatorial
reproductions of the Indians, among whom we the
earliest find the dogma. The real signification of
fire-burial is the commitment of human mortality
into the last-of-all matter, overleaping the inter-
mediate state; or the delivering over of the man-
unit into the Flame-Soul, past all intervening
spheres or stages of the purgatorial: the absolute
doctrine of the Bhudds, taught, even at this day,
among the *Initiates* all over the East. Thus we see
how classic practice and heathen teaching may be
made to reconcile,—how even the Gentile and Hebrew, the mythological and the (so-called) Christian,
doctrine harmonize in the general faith—founded
in Magic. That Magic is indeed possible is the
moral of our work.

"We find, therefore, in the earliest ages, an
AEther (spiritual fire) theory, by which many modern theorists endeavor to explain the phenomena
of magnetism. This is the "*AEtheraem*" of Robert
Fludd, the Rosicrucian.

"Fire, indeed, would appear to have been the
chosen element of God. In the form of a flaming
"bush" He appeared to Moses on Mount Sinai.
His presence was denoted by torrents of flame,
and in the form of fire He preceded the band of
Israelites by night through the dreary wilderness;
which is perhaps the origin of the present custom
of the Arabians, "who always carry fire in front of

their caravans."—(Reade's *Veil of Isis*). All the early fathers held God the Creator to consist of a "subtle fire." When the Holy Spirit descended upon the Apostles on the Day of Pentecost, it was in the form of a tongue of fire, accompanied by a rushing wind.

"The personality of Jehovah is, in Scripture, represented by the Material Trinity of Nature:, which also, like the Divine antitype, is of one substance. The primal, scriptural type of the Father is Fire; of the Word, Light; and of the Holy Ghost, Spirit, or Air in motion.* This Material Trinity, as a type, is similiar to the material trinity of Plato; as a type, it is used to conceal the "Secret Trinity." Holy fires, which were never suffered to die, were maintained in all the temples: of these were the fires in the Temple of the Gaditanean Hercules at Tyre, in the Temple of Vesta at Rome, among the Brahmans of India, Among the Jews, and principally among the Persians.

"As soon as Jesus was born, according to the Gnostic speculative view of Christianity, Christos, uniting himself with Sophia (Holy Wisdom); descended through the seven planetary regions, assuming in each an analogous form to the region, and concealing his true nature from its genii whilst he attracted into himself the sparks of Divine Light they severally retained in their angelic essence. Thus Christos, having passed through the seven *Angelic Regions* before the "THRONE,"

---

*See "Divine Alchemy."

entered into the man Jesus, at the moment of his baptism in the Jordan. From that time forth, being supernaturally gifted, Jesus began to work miracles. Before that, he had been completely ignorant of his mission. When on the cross, Christos and Sophia left his body, and returned to their own sphere. Upon his death, the two took the man "Jesus," and abandoned his material body to the earth; for the Gnostics held that the true Jesus did not (and could not) physically suffer on the cross and die, but that Simon of Cyrene, who bore his cross, did in reality suffer in his room: "And they compel one Simon a Cyrenian, who passed by, coming out of the country, the father of Alexandria and Rufus, to bear his cross" (St. Mark xv. 21.)

The Gnostics contended that a portion of the real history of the Crucifixion was never written.

Asserting that a miraculous substitution of persons took place in the great final act of the "Crucifixion," the Gnostics maintained that the "Son of God" could not suffer physically upon the cross, the apparent sufferer being human only.

"At the point of the miraculous transference of persons, Christos and Sophia (the Divine) left his body, and returned to their own heaven. Upon his death on earth, the two withdrew the "Being" Jesus (spiritually), and gave him another body, made up of ether (Rosicrucian *AEtheraeum*). Thence forward he consisted of the two Rosicrucian principles only, soil and spirit; which was the cause that the disciples did not recognize him after the resurrection. During his sojourn upon earth eighteen

months after he had risen, he received from Sophia
(*Soph*, *Suph*,) or Holy Wisdom, that perfect knowledge or illumination, that true "Gnosis," which he
communicated to the small number of the Apostles who were capable of receiving the same.

"As the Son of God remained unknown to the
world, so must the disciple of Basilides also remain
unknown to the rest of mankind. As they know
all this, and yet must live amongst strangers. therefore must they conduct themselves towards the
rest of the world as invisible and unknown. Hence
our motto, "Learn to know all, but keep thyself unknown." (*Irenaeus*.)

"Though fire is an element in which eveything
inheres, and of which it is the life, still, according
to the Rosicrucian idea, it is itself another element,
in a second non-terrestrial element, or inner, non-
physical, ethereal fire, in which the first coarse fire,
so to speak, flickers, waves, brandishes, and spreads
floating—like a liquid—now here, now there. The
first is the natural, material, gross fire, with which
we are familiar, contained in a celestial, unparticled,
and surrounding medium (or celestial fire), which
is its MATRIX, and of which, in this human body,
we can know nothing.*

"Ptha is the emblem of the Eternal Spirit from
which everything is created. The Egyptians represented it as a pure ethereal fire which burns forever, whose radiance is raised far above the planets and stars. In early ages, the Egyptians wor-

---

*See "Divine Alchemy."

shipped this highest being under the name of Athor.
He was the Lord of the Universe. The Greeks
transformed Athor into Venus, who was looked
upon by them in the same light as Athor. "According to the Egyptians," says Jablonski, "Matter has always been connected with the mind. The
Egyptian priests also maintained that the gods appeared to man, and that spirits communicated with
the human race." The Souls of men are, according to the oldest Egyptian doctrine, formed of
Ether, and at death return again to it."

"The saffron robe of Hymen is of the color of the
Flame of Fire. The Bride, in ancient days, was
covered with a veil called the "*Flammeun;*" unless
made under this, no vow was considered sacred.
The ancient swore, not by the altar, but by the
flame of fire *which was upon the altar.* Yellow, or
Flame-colored, was the color of the Ghebers, or
Guebres, or Fire-Worshippers. *The Persian lilies
are yellow*; and here will be remarked a connection
between this fact of the yellow of the Persian lilies
and the Mystic symbols in various parts. Mystic
rites, and the symbolical lights which mean the
Divinity of Fire, abound at Candlemasday, (February 2nd), or the Feast of Purification; in the torches borne at weddings, and in the typical flame-
brandishing at marriage over almost all the world;
in the illumination at feasts; in the lights on, and
set about the Christian altar; at the festival of the
Holy Nativity; in the ceremonies at preliminary
espousals; in the Bale, or Baal, fires on the summits of the mountains; in the watch-lights, or votive

sanctuary-lights, in the hermitage in the lowest valley; in the *Chapelle Ardente*, in the Romish funeral observances, with its abundance of silent, touching lights around the splendid *Catafalque*, or twinkling, pale and ineffectual, singly at the side of the death-bed in the cottage of the peasant. Starry lights and innumerable torches at the stately funeral, or at any pompous celebration, mean the same. In short, light all over the world, when applied to religious rites, and to ceremonial, whether in the ancient or in the modern times, bespeaks the same origin, and struggles to express the same meaning, which is Parseeism, perseism, or the worship of the Deified *fire*, disguised in many theological or theosophic forms. It will, we trust, never be supposed that we mean, in this, *real fire*, but only the inexpressible something of which real fire, or rather its flower or glory (bright Light), is the farthest off—because, in being visible at all, it is the grossest and most inadequate image.

"The Rosicrucians held that, all things visible and invisible having been produced by the contention of light with darkness, the earth has denseness in its innumerable heavy concomitants downwards, and they contain less and less of the original Divine Dight as they thicken and solidify the grosser and heavier in matter. They taught nevertheless, that every object, however stifled or delayed in its operation, and darkened and thickened in the solid blackness at the base, yet contains a certain possible deposit, or jewel, of light,—which light, although by natural process it may take ages to evolve, as light will tend at last by its own native, irresistible force upward (when it has opportunity), can be liberated; that dead matter will yield this spirit in a space more or less expeditious by the art of the Alchemist. These are worlds within worlds,—we, human organisms, only living in a deceiving, or Bhuddistic, "dream like phase" of the grand panorama. Unseen and unsuspected (because in it lies magic), there is an inner magnetism, or divine *aura*, or ethereal spirit, or possible eager fire, shut and confined, as in a prison, in the body, or in all sensible solid objects, which have more or less of spiritually sensitive life as they can more successfully free themselves from this ponderable, material obstruction. Thus all minerals, in this spark of light, have the rudimentary possibility of plants and growing organisms; thus all plants have rudimentary sensitives, which might (in the ages) enable them to perfect and transmute into locomotive new creatures, lesser or higher in their grade, no nobler or meaner in their functions; thus all plants and vegetables might pass off (by side-roads) into more distinguished highways, is it were, of independent, completer advance, allowing their original spark of light to expand and thrill with higher and more vivid force, and to urge forward with more abounding, informed purpose—all wrought by planetary influence, directed by the unseen spirits (or workers) of the Great Original Architect, building His *microcosmos* of a world from the plans and power evoked in the *macrocosm*, or heaven of first forms, which in their multitude and

magnificence, are as changeable shadows cast off
from the Central Immortal First Light, whose rays
dart from the centre to the extremest point of the
universal circumference. It is with terrestrial fire
that the alchemist breaks or sunders the material
darkness or atomic thickness, all visible nature
yielding to His furnaces, whose scattering heat
(without its sparks) breaks all doors of this world's
kind.

"It is with immaterial fire (or ghostly fire) that
the Rosicrucian loosens contradiction and error,
and conquers the false knowledge and the deceiving
senses which bind the human soul as in its prison.
On this side of his powers, on this dark side (to the
world) of his character, the alchemist (rather now
become the Rosicrucian) works in visible light, and
is a Magician. He lays the bridge (as the Pontifex,
or Bridge-Maker) between the world possible and
the world impossible; and across this bridge he
leads the votary out of his dream of life into his
dream of temporary death, or into extinction of the
senses and of the powers of the senses; which
world's blindness is the only true and veritable
life, the envelope of flesh falling metaphorically off
the now liberated glorious *entity*—taken up, in
charms, by the invisible fire into rhapsody, which
is at the gate of Heaven.

"Now a few words as to the theory of Alchemy.
The alchemists boasted of the powers, after their
elimination and dispersion of the ultimate elements
of bodies by fire (represented by the absent difference of their weights before and after their disso-

11

lution), to recover them back out of that exterior, unknown world surrounding this world: which world men reason against as if it had no existence, when it has real existence. It is this other world (just off this real world) into which the Rosicrucians say they can enter, and bring back, as proofs that they have been there, the old things (thought escaped), metamorphosed into new things. This act is *transmutation*. This product is Magic gold, or "fairy gold," condensed as real gold. This growing gold, or self-generating and multiplying gold, is obtained by invisible transmutation (and in other light) in another world out of this world; immaterial to us creatures of limited faculties, but material enough, farther on, on the heavenly side, or on the side *opposite* to our human side. In other words, the Rosicrucians claimed not to be bound by the limits of the present world, but to be able to pass into this next world (inaccessible only in appearance), and to be able to work in it, and to come back safe out of it, bringing their trophies with them, which were gold, obtained out of this master-circle, or outside elementary circle, different from ordinary life, though enclosing it; and the *elixir vitae*, or the means of the renewal or the perpetuation of human life through this universal, immortal medicine, or *Magisterium*, which being a portion of the light outside, or Magic, or Breath of the Spirits,* fleeing from man, and only to be won in the audacity of alchemical exploration, was independent of those mastered natural elements, or nutritions, necessary to common life.

"The Vedas describe the Persian religion (Fire-
worship) as having come from Upper Egypt.   "The
mysteries celebrated within the recesses of the
"hypogea" (caverns or labyrinths) "were precisely
of that character which is called Fremasonic* or
Cabiric.   The signification of this latter epithet is,
as to written letters, a desideratum.   Selden has
missed it; so have Origen and Sophocles.   Strabo,
to, and Montfaucon, have been equally astray.
Hyde was the only one who had any idea of its composition when he declared that "It was a *Persian
word,* somewhat altered from *Gabri,* or *Guebri,* signifying FIRE-WORSHIPPERS."   Pococke, in his
"*India in Greece,*" is very sagacious and true in his
arguments; but he tells only half the story of the
myths in his supposed successful divestment of
them of all unexplainable character, and of exterior
supernatural origin.   He supposes that all the
mystery must necessarily disappear when he has
traced and carefully pointed out, the identity and
transference of these myths from India into Egypt
and into Greece, and their gradual spread westward.   But he is wholly mistaken; and most other
modern explainers are equally mistaken.

"This is not an attempt to restore to Superstition
its dispossessed pedestal, *but to replace the Supernatural upon its abdicated throne.*   Also to discover
what the nature of this *Fire* should be, which seems
to have been the thing earliest worshipped in the
world, and continued traces of which worship survive not only over all Europe, but in all other countries.   *Fire Philosophy* is the foundation of *all* religions, it is the *very* philosophy of the Soul, of Love
and of God.   Without Fire there could be no existence.   God, Love and the Soul are all the one and
same thing—the *Living Fire.*

Atlantis

Its Beauty.   Its Fall.

"ON that portion of the maps of the earth's surface named the Western Hemisphere can be
found an immense island-studded sea, and an almost
land-locked gulf.   Into this gulf stretches a nearly
perfect parallelogram, the peninsula of Yucatan.

"So long ago that history fades into the hoary
mists of tradition, the gulf was an inland lake.
Where the islands now show themselves amid the
blue waters, a continent sunned itself in the light
of blazing days.

"This continent was peopled by the Aryan race.
Its latitude teemed with all needed conditions to
make exotic life most desirable, whether such life was
on the animal or vegetable plane.   The population increased and multiplied until the whole broad land
became one vast city.   Temples and palaces, works
of skill and art, abounded everywhere.   These did
not there represent the slow toil of human sweat
and agony, of brute force tyrannized into sulky
compliance.   Brilliant in design and bold in execu-
cution, they were the manifestation of *soul-power*
over Elemental force.   The worship of the one God
was taught.   To those who desired, training for
the acquisition of the most Occult and Mystical
knowledge ever known to men was possible.

"They who had charge of these departments as Keepers of the Keys and treasuries of knowledge were neither unaware or regardless of the fact of other planes of existence upon the earth. For thousands of years they strove earnestly to better all states of their fellowmen by imparting a knowledge of the truth.

"By the *silent thought* the whole people were lifted grade by grade as rapidly as they could assimilate the instructions which are of so much influence and assistance in the duties and pleasures of life. Just as fast as they could be educated to perceive these facts, they were advanced in the scale of existence.

"It is true of all peoples, nations, kindreds and tongues, that in proportion as the lower classes rise from a given starting point towards the Light, the force generated (vibrations set in motion) by their action will lift those who are sensitive and fit still farther above them. It is better to be the wise men of a nation of Philosophers than the learned of a race of cringing slaves.

"It is not strange, therefore, that these of whom I speak should have held the mightiest secrets of the universe in their keeping. It was not strange that the trackless waste of water in unknown seas became to them familiar paths, nor that the mysteries of the earth, of the air and of all Nature were at their command. The archives of all ancient nations, carved in their books of stone, speak clearly and truly of them. In Egypt, in Assyria, in India, are found the same inscriptions, conveying the same knowledge, that is to-day locked up in the ruined cities covered by the forests of thousands of years in Yucatan.

'"The western lamp of knowledge was never lighted from the east. From the proud seagirt continent of Atlantis went forth, as from the sun, to all parts of the earth under the heavens, the Illumination of truth and knowledge.

"The old Atlantians, going forth in their galleys hither and yon, so controlled the Elementals by their knowledge of the Hidden Laws of Nature that they had no need to wait for the moving of the winds nor tides. Like Christos, who, in the storm, stilled the waves and bade them be at peace, and immediately they were at the place whither they were going, so the Atlantians moved over the wide wilderness of waters on earth, scattering the seeds of their knowledge along the shores they visited. The seeds fell into good ground in Egypt, Caldea and India.

"It can be noted wherever the pressure of the ever-recurring demands of the physical—that never-yielding circle of necessity—was least on the matter over which the spirit sought to maintain dominion, meanwhile sinking deeper and deeper into its illusions with the downward rush of the cycle, there the seeds of Truth took root and grew most vigorously. At such points were more leisure, strength and purpose to bring forth, as fruit, the knowledge of the unseen in its greatest perfection and abundance. Spirit domination is a tropical fruit reaching mature perfection only in those countries where the bountiful earth ministers voluntarily, always anticipating man's physical necessities, *sun-cooked food does not stimulate groveling desires.*

"The dwellers in more rigorous latitudes, who, in spite of opposing force, still gain spiritual elevation for themselves, are richer in strength and force. This is the result of the discipline acquired in the overcoming of the natural obstacles of their environment. *The harder the battle the more important the victory.* So long as Atlantis obeyed the law that makes all men gods in wisdom, so long it prospered mightily. But there came at last a time when they who had the knowledge only in trust, permitted themselves to think, to wish and to plan for grasping the *absolute control of the whole world.* In this they sought to climb into the seat and place of the Supreme. *Beyond the earth lies only the universe. The lesser is but the result of the greater.*

"The One denies no one knowledge. Whoever seeks to take from it, its authority, its supremacy, thus attempting arrogation or absorption into the Oneness *in any other than the appointed ways which lie open to all created beings, shows a taint of grossness inspiring the desire, surely provocative of swift destruction.* They who thus planned were powerful far beyond the conception of the mortal, holding at their option all the secrets of Nature save one, that one embracing the Infinite supremacy of the one.

"These leaders had freely scattered knowledge abroad upon the earth. By *self denial* and *long training* they had attained, and yet at almost the su-

preme moment, dazzled by the brightness of the
Illumination, they looked once again toward self.
From their memories faded out the unchanging
law; '*Thus far and no farther, shalt thou go.*' The
ceaseless breaking of the waves of the mighty sea
against the silent resistance of rock-bound coasts,
ceased to utter its warning to dazed mentality.
The on-coming day, beginning of the end to those
who had forgotten the very life and essence of the
One, was at hand.   The proud city of Atlantis, city
and continent one, sitting as a queen upon the
throne of the waters, had, by arrogant presump-
tion, filled full the cup of wrath, for which expiation
must be made.   They—masters of all the Elements
and all lawful knowledge of the Unseen—now
sought the *forbidden*, as if the part should demand
equality with the whole.   Step by step they had
reached the veil separating them from the white-
ness of the Immediate Presence; and now, as the
last *fatal* step, they had determined by the exercise
of their most potent skill to rend the veil and come
unheralded and unsummoned before the fact of It
whom no man hath seen at any time.

"Carefully were their preparations made, most
accurately were the sacred computations wrought
out to decide the auspicious hour. . . . . Panoplied
with the consciousness of *previous* achievement,
their call to the embattled hosts of the universe
rang out along the astral currents.   Confidently
the word of power was spoken in all the pride of
human will.   The expected accomplishment did not
follow.   To their amazed horror they discerned a

new vibration, a resultant of creative thought in
its own defence. To this they had no key, and
first bewildered, then terrified, they perceived
that the immense force momentarily by their own
act, had destroyed the accurate balance and adjust-
ment of Nature's laws. Utterly without resource,
they waited for the outcome.

"Thus knowing the *inner*, behold the outer. The
sun rises in its eastern splendor. The mighty millions who dwell in palaces and temples, in luxury
and frugality, dream not of nor can they understand
the word of the Omnipotent, already spoken and
gone forth whereunto it was sent. They awake to
their life of ease and pleasure with the self-assur-
ance that the thing existing hitherto will still continue to be. In their hearts they say: 'Have we
not compelling power and force? Sufficient for the
day is the evil thereof.' They pass on, without
concern, to their usual affairs. Clouds begin to in-
terrupt the clearness of the sky. They deepen
and darken. The uncontrollable, elemental storm
of the tropics, after years of durance, has burst
its prisoning fetters. The people are awed by the
terrific intensity of the outburst, but comfort their
hearts with the idea that it will pass on as it has
hitherto done. They know not that the sceptre
had slipped from the hands of the former rulers,
who, within the chambers of the Three, Five and
Seven, in the great tower of the temple, now lie
prone upon their faces, heroically awaiting the un-
rolling of the book of just judgement. The cyclone
becomes a continuous storm of day after day. The

rocking earth vibrates beneath their feet, and
trembles with each new blast of the mighty forces
of Nature, wind enveloped, drawn here by human
will, and now uncontrolled. The waters of the sea
invade the land. Lashed on by the fierce currents
upon their surface, the tides seem to be mounting
higher and higher. It is now known that it was
the sinking of the the land, and not the rising of
the water, which for ages has hidden from investigation the abodes of the richest and most powerful
nation ever dwelling upon the earth. Foot by foot
all that had ever been given to us by the waters
was again demanded, and returned to its origin.
The records of thousands of years were buried be
neath the storm-tossed waters—buried, but not
destroyed. Only the mountain-tops and the highest plateaus now known as islands, remained of all
the vast continent. The inland lake mingled its
waters with the incoming torrent from the salty
ocean, and a great gulf waters the southern shore
of the country, where now live in peace and wonder, over the hidden past, *the same reincarnated
mighty race.* A few scattered books, written in
stone, were saved, and a wall invisible and imperme-
able, was built around the indestructible manuscript. Unseen and Infinite Power has thus preserved useful knowlede until the times for the re-
vealing shall have come.
  "Fear and dread for ages and ages after the awful cataclysm, detained within the boundaries of
their own country, the feeble remnant of a people
once so invincible and venturesome. The rest of
the world passed on and forgot them.

"The story of the Light bearer who fell from heaven is the story of lost Atlantis.   The legend of the great flood is the true narrative of facts of whose awfulness only the Atlantians had experience. They were forbidden to return to earth until the impetus of their knowledge should in some manner have spent itself, lest recurring memory tempt them to their own future pain.   Thanks to the Ruler of Men, they are again to be permitted to pass out of the valley of that shadow into the possibility of new experience, life and knowledge.   None but he who has lived under the awful shadow can understand what it is to exist outside of the Love currents of the universe, enveloped in the separating displeasure of the Almighty.   Such is *the condition of those who seek selfish interest in preference to the good and pleasure of others.*

"Such is the story of the lost Atlantis, a world in which men had reached earthly perfection, in which all power was given to them but the power to stand face to face with God.   This they could not do nor can any man.   They were not satisfied with their mighty power and as is the case with many Masters of the present day, they try to rend the veil that separates them from the mighty presence of God, and—ruin and absolute loss of power is the result.   The story of Atlantis is to be a warning to all of those who would travel the Occult pass. 'Thus far and no farther, may thou go.'   It is well that all men should be careful for what purpose they use the power after they are once master of it, once they use it for selfish purposes, all is lost.

"In our present incarnation we study to recall the ancient teachings and methods of use in our unfolding, knowing that we gathered from out the 'Golden Age' the 'One Word, One Principle, One Truth,' which will last as long as Eternity. Yet, in each incarnation, we must recall the wisdom already gained, and add new experiences as we continue in the grand march of evolution. Therefore the *new* is built out of the *old*, and who knows but what we shall find some things that will prove the part we played in the drama of life on the stage where the light first appeared in Atlantis, and where it disappeared to reappear in Egypt, flourishing for a time, but finally disappearing in India, leaving that great nation and its people in darkness.

Who knows but in turning to the great Past, studying the ancient people and religions, we may regain some forgotten knowledge to give us the power to reach the place that God intended, when the 'Word became flesh.'

"There is but little revealed concerning the Art of Atlantis. A great deal can be said of the arts of ancient Egypt. Indian history tells us that the degree of excellence attained by that grand nation was of the most exalted kind.

"Art as well as nations, plays a part in the history of progress, and we might say, in many respects of the human mind; for the mode of expression is at all times a type, or symbol, of the tone or feeling which suggests it. In this, the Past is linked with the present. Many consider all efforts in Art or life a sort of influence toward the perfect

Ideal. Therefore, the genius displayed in those days exhibits results more beautiful and perfect than that which came after that era.

"All nations have their Arts, Sciences, and Religions. They display magnificent temples, and palaces where the multitude can gather, giving offerings of physical, as well as spiritual nature to the Deity. The Arts of the ancients were controlled by, or dependent upon, their respective religions, and flourished more or less according to the liberty allowed the Artist and the state of respect in which he was held by his fellowman.

"Little can be traced concerning the Arts and Sciences of Atlantis, therefore allow me to quote something that has been revealed. Our own race, the Aryan, has naturally achieved far greater results in almost every direction than the Atlantians. Where they failed to reach our level, the records of what they did accomplish are of interest as representing the high-water mark which their tide of civilization reached. On the other hand, the character of the scientific achievements in which they did outstrip us are of so dazzling a nature that we are bewildered by such unequal development.

"The Arts and Sciences, as practiced by the first two Races, were, of course, crude in a degree. The history of the Atlantians, as of the Aryan race, was interspersed with periods of progress and decay. Eras of culture were lost in lawlessness, during which their artistic and scientific development was lost: being succeeded by civilization reaching to still higher levels.

"Architecture, sculpture, painting and music were all cultivated in Atlantis. From what has been gathered from nations in the near Past in regard to the development of Music, we cannot expect that the Atlantians reached to any degree of perfection. Their instruments undoubtedly were of the most primitive type; the music at the best was crude.

"One thing is certain, that the Atlantians were fond of color, and brilliant hues decorated both inside and outside of their buildings, but painting as we know it to-day as a fine art could hardly have been established. As time brought forth development of a love for studying Nature and depicting her beauties upon paper, or whatever material they used, drawing and painting must have formed a part of their school studies.

"Sculpture, on the other hand, was most certainly taught to a very great extent and widely practiced. It reached great excellence, becoming in a religious way the custom for the rich to place in some of the temples an image of themselves. These were usually carved in wood, or a black stone. The wealthiest had their statues cast in one of the precious metals, gold, silver, or aurichalcum. This metal was made from a yellow copper ore. Its lustre is pearly; its color pale green, sometimes azure.

"Architecture was naturally widely practiced, as manifesting their respect and devotion to their religious beliefs, if we were to judge, believing as we do that the Atlantians in fleeing from their disappearing country, found a resting place in Egypt. The Atlantians must have built massive structures of gigantic proportions. Their temples were beyond description, but some of the buildings in the last World's Fair in Chicago were built from some remaining memory in the minds of the architects. The future still holds the reproduction of other great temples. As time rolls on and the human family becomes more harmonious and cultured by the refining process of the Spirit, again the 'One Word, One Principle and One Truth' shall dominate forcing through the spirit of harmonious vibration the desire for *one* Church or Temple, the Temple of Universal Brotherhood. This would call for the magnificent structures of the far distant Past. But a greater sense of beauty would be marked as a gift from the ages of training, and simplicity would be the key note.

"The history of Art in Egypt, which is a continuing history of Atlantis, may be divided into two periods, each subject to various changes and revolutions. What took place during the reign of Hyksos, or Shepard Kings, and during the period of the Israelites' captivity, or the immediate generations preceding the eighteenth dynasty, or that of Rameses the Great, who lived about fourteen centuries before the birth of the Master, Jesus of Nazareth, may be considered the first beginning of Egyptian Art, of whice we know nothing beyond what is said in the book of Genesis and the account in Exodus. Both must be understood in their literal sense.

"Pliny tells us, according to their own accounts,

the Egyptians were masters of painting full 6,000 years before it passed from them to the Greeks. The Art of Egypt was purely symbolic in its principles and historic in its practice; and was the tool of a hierarchy and its artists the slaves of superstitions. Egyptian hieroglyphics appear to be simply records, social, religious, and political. Egyptian painting was accordingly more of a symbolical writing than a liberal art.

"The architectual remains that have attracted so much notice in Egypt during the last century are scattered along both sides of the Nile, for a distance of nearly a thousand miles. They consist of temples, pyramids, obelisks and monoliths or large stone pillars. Very discordant opinions have been expressed as to the periods when these various monuments were built, but it is generally agreed that their construction must have embraced the long period of at least 2,000 years. Some, situated near the mouth of the Nile, having been constructed after the commencement of the Christian era; while others, high up in the country toward Abyssinia, are believed to have been built nearly 2,000 years before the Christian era. Whatever may be the difference of opinion on these conjectural points, it is agreed by those who *know*, that Egypt displayed the most mighty examples of structures which were built ages before Greece and Rome were numbered among the nations of the world, and that all other ancient structures may be best viewed by comparing them with those of Egypt.

"At a short distance from Denderah, now called

12

upper Egypt, is the most extraordinary group of
architectural ruins presented in any part of the
world, known as the Temples of the ancient City
of Trebes. Trebes in its prime occupied a large
area on both sides of the Nile. This city was the
center of a great commercial nation of Upper Egypt,
ages before Memphis was the capital of the second
nation in Lower Egypt; and however grand the architectural monuments of the latter may have been,
those of the former must have surpassed them.

"What sublime conceptions can be derived from
such magnificent specimens of man's creation in
architecture, not only in magnitude, but in form,
proportion, and construction. The portrayal by
pencil or brush can convey but a faint idea of the
perfected city. As the city stands to-day it is like
a city of giants, who after a long conflict, have been
all destroyed, leaving the ruins of their various
temples as the only proofs of their existence.

"The Temple of Luxor (it was in this temple that
the Grand Lodge of Initiates always met) stands on
a raised platform of brickwork covering more than
2,000 feet in length and 1,000 in breadth. It is the
one that interests the members of all Ancient Orders, especially so all the members of those Orders
that worshipped at the Shrine of the *Secret Fire*,
more than perhaps any other, and stands on the
eastern bank of the Nile. It is in a very ruined
state, but records say the stupendous scale of its
porportions almost takes away the sense of its in-
completeness. Up to about a quarter of a century
ago, the greater part of its columns in the interior,

and part of the inner sanctuary remained, but the outer walls had been removed after falling, for use elsewhere.

"This Temple (which figures more or less in the history of the different Occult or Mystical Orders as all originally come from one source and that source Atlantis, from the Atlantian Fire Worshippers), was founded by Amenothis III, who constructed the southern part, including the heavy colonnade over-looking the river; but the world is indebted to Rameses II for the remaining portion, but destruction unfortunately conceals this fact. The chief entrance to the Temple looked to the East; while the Holy Chamber at the upper end of the plan approached the Nile. As mighty as the Temple of Luxor, seems to have been, it was exceeded in magnitude and grandeur by that of Carnak. The distance between these two great structures was a mile and a half. Along this avenue was a double row of Sphinxes placed twelve feet apart and the width of the avenue was sixty feet. When in perfect state, this avenue must have presented the most extraordinary entrance that the world has ever seen. If we had the power to picture from the field of imagination the grand processions of Neophytes that were constantly passing through and taking part in the ceremonies of Initiation, we would be powerless to produce the grandeur of the surroundings and the imposing sight of color and magnificent trappings of those who took part. Neither can we produce the music that kept the vast number of people in steady marching order.

Crude it may have been to the cultivated ear of the twentieth century. But could not the palpitating strain sung by massed voices on the lapse of time, whose history touches the profoundest aspirations of the human heart, like the trend of a mighty river, become the grand currents of Universal Law, imparting the desire of that shadowy Past, as it steps forth from the pages of a history dim with age?

"Egypt must have been, when these Temples were built, a material nation; for records of its warlike deeds are perpetuated in deeply engraved tablets, which even now, excite the admiration of the best judges of archaeological remains. It was also a highly civilized nation and of a nature that could bear the expenditure which always attends the culture of the Arts. Yet, as strange as it may seem, we do not know with any certainty, either its history or its chronology. It surpassed, in its astonishing architecture, all other nations that have existed upon the earth and yet the greater power and beauty which belongs to intellect was scarcely to be traced.

"In those times, the armies of Egypt went forth to conquer and subdue the known *physical* world. But the knowledge and potency that found rest and culture at Atlantis, Luxor, and Elephantis, so permeated and controlled all nations that records of experience, becoming knowledge, have been preserved even to the present day. So deeply were they impressed upon the *unseen*, that they returning upon their cycles of development, have been considered by our age, as original inventions and

discoveries. The earth-born forget nothing so
easily as wisdom, or its possession. The Thrice-
Wise said: 'There is nothing new under the sun.'
But in our day, when instead of the best men and
soldiers of a nationality coming forth from fair and
beautiful cities, arrayed for the conquest, the armies of Egypt and Chaldea are swarming from out
the *unseen*. They are overruning all countries
where there is spiritual Light and Life enough to
give them assurance of sufficient advancement to
warrant their incarnation. They are hampered by
the customs and restrictions of the mortal laws,
and their own strict regard for all law. If there
was one thing more than another that an Egyptian
respected and venerated, it was the law under
which he lived; the symbols of authority upon the
throne; and the sign of Spiritual Presence in the
temple. Urged on, however, by the impulses of
the Higher Self, they are striving in this day and
generation to the best of their unfolding, for their
own progress, and for the consolidation of the
Brotherhood seen and *unseen*. They have perceived it was absolutely necessary to rise above the
mental impediments of their environments, and the
unseen brotherhood who are not yet ready to support their colleagues, in manifestation, stand behind
them rank upon rank. The impulse and the vibration coming from these supporting columns, thrill
along the soul formations of the past. The vibrations bring recurring memories, which whisper of
the One, the great God *Om*, and of His truth.
Everywhere, on all lines, these Ancient Ones are

seeking to verify in the outer, what Cabalistic symbols and signs are, the Hidden Truths of Being,
which from time to time have been whispered out
of the intelligence and knowledge locked up in the
Archives of the Astral Light Library.

"Oh! You Neophytes, listen to the Voice that
comes out of the Silence, and believe it for the
truth's sake. You have not yet concentrated
enough. The Watch-Fire on the mountain top do
not yet break down the darkness. So separated
they contain within themselves, weakness. If they
can be brought together, knowing each other's feeling and intensity of purpose, which demands sacrifice of the modes of expression, of the spirit of
the utterances, then it will be as if a thousand camp-
fires were massed in one, and it became the beacon
light of the world. The field is ripe for the harvest
and the stalks are falling on the ground from the
weight of the grain; will you save it? Will you accomplish for yourself that which shall make the
path of those who follow you easier? We have, in
our Archives, the Mysteries, are you ready to receive them? As Egypt in the olden time, when her
star of glory was the highest, was mistress of the
world, so now may you be full of potency and power, Masters of the good, ready to lead on and place
on record the conditions needed to bring about the
opening again of that which was lost to those who are
now crying, hungering, and thirsting for the truth.

"The true Egyptian knows whatever was lost,
has not disappeared, in the sense of being destroyed,
but is simply veiled. The Veil of Isis is thrown

over it, and no arm since that time, has been strong enough, potent enough, *will*-ful enough to tear it aside.   The land of Egypt lies desolate, the stranger treadeth within her gates, desolation broods over her temples, her palaces, her cities, and the Archives and treasures of Incomparable knowledge. How long, O sons of Egypt! Brothers of the one family!   Sons of the One! will you refuse or think it of little moment to take concerted and united action, that there may come to Light once again all the beauty and grandeur; all the potency and knowledge that have been waiting thousands of years, for the time and times when you should once more be upon earth.   *We, in our Secret Archives hold the documents and the Mysteries of the temples.   Are you ready to receive these Mysteries?   Shall the cycles move on, and you having accomplished your pilgrimage, go hence into the Unseen leaving all unrevealed that might have come to you; and thus all the world to await the unfolding of another cycle?   You are face to face with all that ever has been.   The means are in your hands; the world is before you; the potencies of the most ancient knowledge with the direct influence of the search-light pouring upon it is your birthright.   Take and use it. Commence at once and persist, until you have reached that point where you can say to the physical, stay, as I shall have need of thee.*

"Egypt has left us no memory of a Homer, a Pericles, a Plato, or a Xenophon. A single Hebrew writer, Moses, gives us a clearer insight, a more exact and truthful view of the actual state of that land than we can gain from any of its monuments,

or written remains, or from Herodotus or any other
Greek.   The chief idea presented to us in the rapid
sketches of the book of Moses, is that of *power*—
absolute power.   'I am Pharaoh, and with me none
shall lift up his hands or foot in all the land of Egypt.'
All travelers on their journeys stand amazed at all
the prodigies which surroud them on every side,
but the chief fact is the same.   Power, must
have created all these things; for, in the Twentieth
Century of the Christian era, to reproduce the
works which can be found even in the present, at
Luxor and Carnak would be utterly and entirely
impossible.

These powerful works should teach us that without unity and Brotherhood nothing can be done.

*So long as the Atlantians were united and obeyed the
Supreme Law, all was well, but no sooner did they follow the flesh and become dis-united, when the fall came.
This is the history of not only the Atlantians, but also of
the Egyptians.*

So long as we are disunited and self-seeking, we
are creating both the visible and *invisible* realms, a
feeling of opposition that grows stronger and
stronger, as we increase our momentum of individ-
uality.   To this condition, by the very essence of
its existence is necessarily drawn all other discordant forces.   Singly, they hold, perhaps, but little
energy, but like grains of sand, in united action,
can weigh tons.   It is strange how long it has tak-
en man to learn this lesson of unity from the physical world; but as he will not let go of his physical,
and look towards the spiritual side of himself, he

must receive the chastisements that are the inevitable consequence.   When he does come to the time and place, where from the spiritual side of himself, he perceives a new view from his contemplation. This does not help self as a center of action or a starting point of force; but it holds out; it makes unity of harmonious action the main spring of all life.

The "words of the wise" to man, consequently ring and echo with injunctions to him of the important import: "Obey the law—the word of the Supreme Will." "Do the will of the Father." These reiterated words of advice are forever reverberating through the arches of space.   The more we declare we will not obey, but will follow our own short-sighted inclinations in the direction of our desire and pleasure, the more we shall be sure to become tangled in savagery.   Here we run against the immutable law, bringing upon ourselves, the condign punishment or pain, by which only our animality can be trained.   It is we and *not* God who is benefitted by our conformity to law—that natural order of things.   Thus we as animals, have been and are gradually forced to perceive that the potency of united action is the only way by which we may hope to succeed.   To be eminently successful, is the only result if we are truly on the basis of Universal Law, the only right method of action.

Under the impress of the spirit, we become desirous of being of some service to all our fellows, even if it is no more than to eat at the second table. When we have come to this point, it is no longer

possible for us to hold enmity againt our fellows,
even in behalf of our most carefully cultivated feuds.
What others may do, often causes annoyance, but
never that unrelenting setness, we know as hatred,
which like the hardening of a plaster cast, binds
into an immovable and inflexible limitation, influenc-
ing even astral conditions to both the hater and
hated.

The reader may think that I am transgressing
by quoting from *Secret records*, but I am not. In
giving a history of a people or an order, it is necessary to give the cause of their fall so that other Orders or people may take warning from the past and
not fall into the same error as those people of the
past and also to point them the way as to what to do
in order to avoid the downfall.

"It is a mistake to look at an Egyptian Temple in
the light of a Church, or even of a Greek Temple.
Here no public worship is performed; the faithful
do not congregate for public prayer; indeed, no one
is or was admitted inside the Sanctuary except the
Priest and the Initiates of the Order.   In some, not
even the King, unless he was an Initiate, was allowed at all times.   The Temple is a royal prosce-
nium, that is, a token of piety from the King who
erected it in order to deserve the favor of the Gods.

"The Egyptian Temples are always dedicated to
three Gods—a Triad.   The first is the male principle.   Second, the female principle.   Third, the off-
spring of the two.   Creator, creating, and creation.
Thus the three Deities are blended into *one*, expres-
sing no beginning or end.   We thus prove that the

Ancient Mysteries were taught and celebrated
First, in Atlantis; Second, in Egypt; Third, in Elephantis. These proofs we have. In all of the Temples of these places the *Fire Philosophy* was taught
as it has been throughout all the Secret Orders
since the time of Ancient Atlantis. Of the Fire
Philosophy of Atlantis, Egypt and India, not much
can be said in a history as they are secret and not
to be divulged to the profane. Only a small part of
these instructions may be quoted from the secret
manuscript in order to prove that such was the
philosophy of the ancient Masters.

"Each spark contains the *Flame* consciousness
belonging to every soul, which evolves finally into
manifestation. In it, and under all, rests the eternal Essence, the Never-Dying *Flame* which once
lighted, (Soul awakened) bridges the Eternal Past
with the Eternal Future. It is the Life Existent,
the Soul of Fire. *It* is the Only True Way, the Infinite God.

The Mighty Spirit of the *Flame* has no destruc-
tive essence *within* itself. But it holds all power,
by Divine commission, to create the light that
glorifies and uplifts everything that it shines upon.
The central Fire (God) radiates to the circumference and there touches the periphery of *all* its existence. Again returning to the Center, it holds
ensouled *within* its vibrations, other souls to be il-
luminated and become self-radiating from the same
Great *Fire*. The *fire* of all the Gods is kindled from
and concentrated in one Great God!

"Since the beginning of days, sacrifices have

been laid upon the altar of *Fire*. In all ancient writings are we told of the common fire; the sacred *Fire* and of Sacrificial *Fire*. What means the fire upon the altar? What means the Mysterious Light; the incense soaring in misty waves, as a Soul expands in exaltation; the air heavy with its exhaled perfume: the solemn multitude of lamps, which with their richly wrought golden arbra gleams about Shrine and tabernacle? What? But that *Fire*, ascending toward heaven in its pristine blueness and triangular shape, *is the profoundest symbol of the supreme life-giving power.*

"Watching the leaping flame, the Triangle plainly manifests itself. The base below, the apex pointing up, is from the beginning put forth is symbolic of the Unseen, the Unknown God. There is nothing in all the world that holds so completely within itself, all the attributes of the Supreme intelligence. The point reaching upward is always the node of superior energy, the Center of Life and sensation. Hence, the apex of the fiery triangle must be the Absolute, for the real *potency of Fire appears at the moment of contact.*

"*The spirit of Fire we cognize as Life. Wherever God is, there Fire, as the Holy Ghost, will also be. Wherever Fire is, there is Life. Wherever Fire rests, there manifestation will be. If Fire is Life, then it must hold within itself the Divine Intelligence. Hence the flame. The essential essence of the flame is Life—God. If Fire is God and God is Love, the essential Fire must be Love and thus we can only find the fire through Love and God through the fire. The manifested fire can*

*sweep away all man's possession, and destroy his body,
but the Essence dropping into the Secret Place of the Most
High, the maelstrom or vehicle, which holds Within itself
the Unseen charm of all existence, lights the Flame that
makes man Immortal.*

"Where man worships, the lights burning upon
the alter, are symbolical of the Divine Energy, of
generation and regeneration. These flaming lights
encircle the most holy point of the ancient mosques.
They glow in ambient beauty about the Shrine of
saints and the churches of the Eternal Cities. They
burn constantly in Mystic attestation before the
tombs of the Redeemers. Always and everywhere,
they are and always have been, a silent witness and
sign to the Initiate, of the origin and significance
of the Sun Worshippers.

Man seeing fire struck out from the cold, unyield-
ing flint, comes to believe, the coldest, hardest stone
must have a heart of fire. *All Nature is built upon
the Divine Fire.* The flagstone of matter shuts it
down, waiting for the great Central Sun to drop a
ray of fiery essence into the bosom of Mother Earth,
It thereby creates sufficient impulse to cause it to
stream forth, unwind its starry limbs, and step into manifestation. This fire descending upon the
altar of Mother Earth holds concealed as its ultimate, the Secret of Life.

"The lily bulb contains the same forceful fire,
It possesses the Creative Energy to rise from the
lowest to the highest. The Lotus is the whole lesson and law of transmutation. By its own function
and growth the law of the Creative Energy acts.

The gross becomes the supernal. The supreme
atom of the lily and all else that is, has kindled, at
the base of this Altar of the Waters, the Eternal
Essence of Life, which is fire. When it reaches the
surface, in manifesting beauty, there burns *within*
its bosom—White Chalice of the Gods, the *Heart of
Fire*—the tongue of flame of the Holy Spirit. Having descended into matter for the purpose of taking
hold of the material, it *converts* the opaque into the
brilliant purity of the Highest Transmutation. The
Holy Spirit does not really descend, but only places
Itself in touch with that which is lower. What a
beautiful illustration of the True Initiation we have
here. The secret is so plainly unveiled that all who
have eyes may see.

"The fire springing out of the Etheric and Auric
vibrations, is the highest Esoteric Fire, born of the
spontaneous action of the positive and negative
forces. We gaze with awe upon its multiform
shapes; its trails of sparks; its flame wreaths; scin-
tilating, wavering arches and vortices, starting up
out of the matrix of apparent solidity, reducing its
source to its own ultimate *invisibility*.

*Flame is significant of rebirth and Resurrection; of
the Spiritual born out of the material. It is symbol and
substance at once, of the Immortality of the Ego.* Hence
the Angel of Fire hath dominion. Above all, is the
glowing supernatural flower of Love, concealed in
the inanimate womb of matter. The great love of
the physical world, whose warmth and ardor des-
troys the material and perceptible form, is symbolized by the enwrapping flame. Freed from its

prison of limitation and thus formless, it gives rebirth to the spirit, in both the Seen and the Unseen
worlds.

. *"The Fire God, the Beautiful, the Resplendent! Con-
ceived in the Land of Silence! Born out of the womb of
Mystery! Thou art the Shadow of the Shadowless!
Thou art the Causeless Cause! The existent God. We
worship not the Fire, but that which represents the Fire
—Love.*

"There is no power but Love, strong enough to
hold through all the complex problems of earth life.
It is Love that meets us as we cross the threshold
of the narrow gate. It is Love that looks into
our eyes, as we close them in the last earthly sleep.
It is Love that greets us, when the Gates of Para-
dise swing inward for our reception, after our long
or brief pilgrimage in the mortal realm. Love is
that which abides, and is as eternal as God. This
is the Love that dies not. They who love truly, can
easily and cheerfully put aside self for the Beloved.
Whoever returns to earth searching for who he seek,
can only find and rejoin them, by entering into this
realm of Omnipotence. Love is a guide which will
never fail. Love will restore the loved ones to each
other should they ever be lost.

"Love, the Law, in its fulfilling, must hold for itself, both an inflowing and an outflowing current.
The ebb and flow of the life blood, is symbolical of
the give and take of love in activity. He who loves,
lives in the highest realm of the *all-life*. He who
loves counts all things but loss, if he may but win
and hold the true love and real affection of the one

loved. The true lover, takes labor and toil by the
hand, as benefactors and boon companions, leads
them into verdant pastures giving fresh hope to the
tired and overtaxed heart. Love tunes the Harp
of Life to the perfect vibration of the At-One Ment.
When played upon by the hands of Fate and Destiny, and discord made thereby, may be harmon-
ized by the soft, lingering touch of Love, the Divine,
the Perfect Harper!

Listen! All social problems lie in the conquest
over the Natural and personal man. It is the continual protest over the Natural Law. Rising into
the world of Love and self-consciousness, we rise
into a world of freedom and equality. A great
teacher has said: "Man is a composite being. In
him is the angelic and the animal. The spiritual
training of life means no more, *than the subjugation
of the animal; and the setting free of the Angelic.*"

"There is a great and wonderful epitome founded
upon having, and holding in our possession, the
key that unlocks all doors, and the knowledge of
how to use and handle it. *That key is Love.* He who
loves lives; he who loves not, is dead; he who loves
himself alone, lives in hell, because centering all the
essence of existence upon his own body, he burns
and shrivels under the intolerant intensity of its
force. He *who loves others, lives in heaven, because the
desire to love and bring good, reacts and compels harmony.*"

Such are the secret instructions that have come
down to us for ages from the grand temples that
once stood upon the shores of Atlantis. These are

but few of the mighty secrets held in secret crypts
of our sacred Occult Libraries.

The Templars as Fire Philosophers.

The great men and inquiring spirits among the
Templars had penetrated to the very depth of the
mystery of the ever-living, supernatural *Fire* and
had taught it to their Initiates as they had been
taught by the Saracens.   It is supposable that, at
the suppression of this grand, warlike, and monas-
tic Order—so bound by the injunctions of a secret
formula, which, in all the persecutions of the Camps
or Lodges, never appeared to the eyes of the world,
but was denied;—many of the things of which they
were accused, such as Magical ceremonies and so-
called Pagan rites, wizard-trances and sacrifices,
etc., were satisfactorily established (in their trials),
as matters of which they were indisputably guilty.
We know that they had their rites and ceremonies,
but we also know that these rites and ceremonies
had a different meaning from that interpreted by
religious fanatics and self-constituted investigators
who knew nothing of the Deeper Occult Sciences
and who must be called the real Pagans and worshippers of Rome and the golden-calf.

We know that there was nothing more in the de-
nouncement and extinction, at the same time, all
over Europe, of these religio-knightly or monastic-
military orders—in whose ranks fought, and taught,
some men of the most powerful, and most daring,
understanding of the period—than the jealousy of

13

their power, and fear of their influence and the desire of their riches and worldly accumulation. We *know* that secret and forbidden studies (as in all Fraternities) were pursued by them; that under the protection and yet in the refusal (as it seemed to the profane and religious fanatics) of the Cross, and as from behind their holy and militarily wondrous character, the Arch-leaders among them (whether chieftains of mind or of arms) closely hung on the track of philosophy until it vanished into transcendentalism, or the so-called (because so-called religious beliefs were no more accepted by them than they are at this time by the Members of Mystic Fraternities) atheistic, and by Occult and Cabalistic means established relations with the Unseen (as we do to-day), seeking to hold communications with the Spiritual world.

The round form of their Temples—as they were styled by the Brotherhood;—their various *insignia* and habits; their secret Book;—their rites—all seem to bespeak a knowledge, and do so speak to the Initiate, of the true Fire-Philosophy:—misunderstood and perverted in the hands *of all but those, who, of the Order, had risen to the highest knowledge in it—and who rose to truth*—into the indulgence of sensual appetites and the denial of the future life, and, consequently, of the fullest and the morally darkest, though the most worldly luscious epicureanism. This was not the fault of the mighty Philosophy known and taught by them, but the fault of those would be followers who did not try to understand, and who did not desire to follow the true teachings, but who only wanted an excuse for their miserable outrages.

Whilst the chiefs of the Order of the Templars had penetrated to truths the most astonishing though, necessarily, undivulgeable (especially in that superstitious and ignorant age; of which, incontestably, they were far forward), they paid the usual penalty of their great knowledge in being decried, and burnt as magicians. Simply because the time was not prepared—if, indeed, any time can be—for that which they could tell. They, and their whole body, therefore, appeared, in the exaggerations of the Church, and in the magnifying medium of the terror which their doings inspired, as thirsting for seemingly impossible things. Climbing, as in their cowls and mail, as a storming ladder of presumptuously supposed lightning-proof, steel, and under the mask and shield of the Cross, into the imagined, accursed (according to the profane) chambers of the Magic, devilish Fire: the treasure house, or home, or Hell of the forbidden gods, rich in all possible Ethereal and human splendors! The Templars did only that which we, of the present school are doing, only, the masses have become more enlightened and while we may be accused by the ignorant, persecutions are past and we have better learned to be *silent*.

The famous Beauseant, or banner of the Templars, was part-colored—that is, divided down the centre, in two halves of "black and white." This figuring-forth of the utterly opposed colors, is generally taken to signify the immitigable hatred of

the Templars for the Infidels, but their abiding love
and benignity towards the Christians. This total
friendship, or uncompromising abnegation would
be heraldically denoted in the perfect contrast of
the black and white halves, or "fields," of the Templars' ensign, divided *parti-per-pae*. But, when we
remember that the Egyptians mythed their Perfect
Divinity, or Cause of All, under (of this world) the
hopeless, empty color of Black, in opposition to
White, or Matter-Light which was taken to signify
"This World, and the Glory of this World;" and,
when we recall that the proper robes, or vestments,
or Magicians, when invested in their Cabalistic pan-
opy and armed for charms—as directed by the authentic formula—are of the colors White and Black,
we grow into another sort of belief regarding the
meaning of this Templar banner, Mystic as it is,
and we conclude that it fell back, for its *real* hieroglyph, upon the Fire-Creed or Philosophy. This
faith of the fierce Deistical East, and of the Guefre;
Gubh, or Gaur. And this, surely, not without reason. Nor does the Order of the Knights of St. John
of Jerusalem, who, in the grandeur of their stately
galleys, made of the Mediterranean a royal sea,
and elevated the Islands of Malta, and of Rhodes,
almost into the splendors of an empire set on the
water; nor does this Order escape the imputation
of wrong-doing—of being betrayed in the signs and
the hieroglyph of the secret, reprobated, Infidel
doctrine. Their colors, the fashion of their arms,
and their attire, in which—in priestly or any other
orders or communities—lies much of meaning, glanc-

ing up to justifiable Christian suspicion in the wizard, heretical half-light.   In short, it is held that the Teutonic Knights, or the soldier monks, of St. John of Jerusalem, as equally as the Templars, as very questionable Christians.   Though this *imagined* infidelity might be only confined to the Heads of the Chapters: the great body of the Knights being merely directed.

In the persecutions of the Knights Templars, which are generally known, a certain mystification and secrecy may be observed; as if the whole of the charges against them were not brought out publicly. This arose from various causes.   The persecuted were really very religious, and were bound by the most solemn Masonic oaths (and Masonry was intimately connected with these matters) not to divulge the secrets of the Order.   The impression is very general that these persecutions were undertaken for the sake of the wealth of the Order.   This is not the only reason, there were other, and deeper reasons.   Hate, jealousy and fear were of the greatest reasons.

The so-called heathenish doctrines to which allusion has been made, are visible everywhere in the curious mystical figures always seen upon the monuments of the Templars; in the fishes, bound together by the tails, in the tombs of Italy, and appearing on the vaulting of the Temple Church, London;—in the astrological emblems on many churches, such as the Zodiacs on the floor of the Church of St. Irenaeus at Lyons, and on a church at York, and Notre Dame at Paris, and Bacchus, or the God

I. H. S., filling the wine-cask, formerly on the floor
of the Church of St. Denis.   Again, in the round
Churches of the Templars, in imitation of the round
church at Jerusalem, probably built by them in the
Circular, or Cyclar, or Gilgal form, in allusion to
various recondite subjects, and in the monograms
I H E and X H in thousands of places.   We, of the
present day, know that these doctrines were *not*
heathenish in any sense but that they had and still
have, the most' wonderful mystical meaning and
that they figure in all true Initiation and in all the
Philosophies.   Symbolism has never been understood by the masses and ever a strange and absolutely false meaning will be given to these symbols
and ceremonies by those who do not, and never can
understand them.   It is well that this is so.

At every turn we meet with some remnant of so-
called Paganism.   It is a rather extraordinary
thing that the Christian Templars should call themselves Templars in honor of the Temple, the destruction of which all so-called Christians boasted of
as a miraculous example of Divine wrath in their
favor to Christians.   This then, goes to prove the
Templars much older than the Crusades, and that
the pretended origin of these people is totally false.
There is a certain suspicion entertained, not without reason, that the origin of this community may
be looked for in the College of Cashi, and the Temple of Solomon in Cashmere, or the lake, or mere,
of Cashi.   The Gymnosophists, the Kasideans, the
Essenes (from whom the Christ received his Initiation), the Therapeutae (later, and at present, the

Rosicrucians), the Dionesians, the Eleusianians (followers of the Essenes), the Pythagoreans (who
were really Rosicrucians), the Chaldeans were, in
reality, all an order of religionists, who included
in their religion, both Philosophy and true Mysticism. Including among them, who were, in fact,
the heads of the Societies.

The Teutonic Knights seem to have been the first
instituted. But it is thought that they were graften
upon a class of persons—charitable devotees—who
had settled themselves, as the historians say, near
the Temple at Jerusalem, to assist poor Christian
pilgrims who visited it; although the real temple
had dissappeared even to the last stone, for a thousand years. This shows how little use these historians make of their understandings. The Teutonic Knights are said to have come from Germany,
from the Teutonic tribes. Let us hasten to relieve
North Germany from the weighty and undeserved
honor. The word Teut is Tat, and Tat is Buddha.
The name of Buddha, with some of the German nations, was Tuisto or Tuisco, derived from whose
name comes our day of the week—Tuesday. From
Tuisto or Tuisco came the Teutones, *Teutisci*, and
the Teutonic Knights, and the name of Mercury
Teusco. Perhaps, Mercury *Trismegitus*.

The round church of Jerusalem, built by Helena,
the Mystic Helena (daughter of Coilus), mother of
Constantine, who was born at York, and the chap
ter-house at York, and at other cathedrals, were
reproductions of the circular Stonehenge and
Abury. The choirs of many of the cathedrals in

France and England are built crooked of the nave
of the church, for the same reason, whatever that
might be, that the Druidical temple is so built at
Classerniss in Scotland. All the round *chapter-
houses* of our Cathedrals were built round for the
same reason that the Churches of the Templars
were round. In these chapters and the crypts, till
the thirteenth century, the Secret Religion or true
Fire Philosophy was celebrated far away from the
profane vulgar. These buildings have been thought
to be the representative successors of the caves of
India, and afterwards of the cupola-formed buildings there, of the Cyclopean Treasury of Atreus at
Mycenae, and of the Labyrinths of which we read
in Egypt, Crete, Italy and other countries. These
labyrinths could be only for the purposes of religion, and, it is not to be doubted, of that religion of
the Cyclops which universally prevailed. The under ground crypts of our cathedrals, with their forests of pillars, were labyrinths in miniature. There
is something about the circular churches of the
Templars which seem very remarkable. We have
only four in England, we believe, of the churches of
the Templars, namely: those in London, at Maple-
stead in Essex, at Northampton, and at Cambridge
—and they are all round. This form, we are told,
was adopted in imitation of the round church at
Jerusalem. But how came the church at Jerusalem to be round? Perhaps Phallas Worship had
something to do with this form. We are led to believe so at least. Again, how came these Christian
Knights to be called by the name of the detested
Jewish Temple?

The Templars were divided into orders exactly
after the system of the Assassins, Knights, Es-
quires, and Lay-Brethren answered to the Refeck,
Fedavee, and Laseek of the Assassins; as the Prior,
Grand-Prior, and Grand-Master of the former cor-
respond with the Dai, Dai-Al-Kebir, and Sheik of
the mountain of the latter.

As the Ishmaelite Refeck was *clad in white*, with a
red mark of distinction, so the Knight of the Temple
wore a white mantle, adorned with a red mark of
distinction—the *Red Cross*. It is remarkable that
they were called "Illuminators." And it is to be
suspected that the *red* mark of distinction, kept
back as common to both Templers and Ishmaelites,
was red eight-point cross, or a *Red Rose* on a *Cross*.

The Templars were accused of worshipping a being called Bahumid and Bafomet, or Kharuf. Von
Hammer says that this word, written in Arabic,
has the meaning of "Calf," and is what Kircher calls
Anima Mundi. It is difficult not to believe that this
"Kharuf" is our "Calf." The Assassins are said
to have worshipped a Calf. If these latter have a
Calf in use as an emblem, it may be justly considered as a proof that, contrary to the prevailing ideas
concerning them, that they are a tribe of *extreme*
antiquity; (a branch of the Atlantians) which, though
holding the doctrine of the Ten Incarnations, yet
still clings to the ancient worship of Taurus. There
is a picture, in Russia, of the Holy Family, in which
the Calf is found instead of the Ram. A learned
author pronounces that the doctrines of the Assassins and the Templars were the same.

All Temples were surrounded with pillars recording the numbers of the constellations, the signs of the Zodiac, or the cycles of the planets; and each *Templum* was supposed, in some way, to be a microcosm, or symbol, of the Temple of the universe, or of the starry vault called *Templum.* It was this Templum of the universe from which the Knights Templars took their name, and not from the individual Temple at Jerusalem; built probably by their predecessors, and destroyed many years before the time alloted to their rise; but which rise, it is suspected, was only a revivification from a state of depression into which they had fallen.

Theatres were originally Temples, where the *mythos* was scenically represented.   And until they were abused they were intended for *nothing* else. But it is evident that, for this purpose, a peculiar construction of the Temple was necessary.   When Scaurus built a Theatre in Greece, he surrounded it with 360 pillars.   The Temple at Mecca was surrounded with 360 stones.   And, in like manner, with the same number the Templum at Iona, in Scotland, was surrounded.   The Templars were nothing but one branch of Masons, perhaps a branch to which the care of some peculiar part of the Temples was entrusted; and there is probability that the name of Templars was only another name for Casideans.

In the Western part of Asia, in the beginning of the twelfth century, the sect or religious tribe called Ishmaelites, or Battenians, or Assassins, arose. These "Assassins" were first noticed, in the West-

ern world, with their chief Hakem Bermrillah, or
Hakem-biamr-allah, who was held up, in Syria, as
the Tenth Avatar, or, as it is assumed, incarnation.
His ideas of God were very refined. The first of
the creatures of God, the only production *immediate*
of His power, was the *intelligence universelle*, which
showed itself at each of the manifestations of the
Divinity on earth; that by means of this minister,
all creatures were made, and he was the Mediator
between God and man. They called themselves
Unitarians. This *intelligence universelle* is the Logos,
Rasir, or Buddha.

It would seem probable that the followers of Bem-
rillah were originally adorers of Tauras, or the Calf
of Calves, which they continued to mix with the
other doctrines of Buddha. It must be remem-
bered that this worship of the Calf is not to be tak-
en in its literal sense but is only a *symbol* of the
Lamb or Christos. The hidden, *Living Fire* indwelling in all men and coming from God—*Love*.

Chaldean implies Sabaean. (Another sect of Fire
worshippers or Fire Philosophers.) The word
Chaldean is a corruption of the word Chasdim; and
this is most clearly the same as the Colida, and Col-
chida, and Colchis of Asia, and as the Colidei and
Culdees of Scotland. Now all this, and the circumstances relating to the Chaldees, often called Math-
ematici, to the Assassins, the Templars, Manicha-
eans, etc., being considered, the name of the Assassins, or Hassessins, or Assanites, or Chasiens, or
Alchaschisin, will not be thought unlikely to be a
corruption of Chasdim, and to mean Chaldees or

Culdees, and that they were connected with the Templars. We can thus trace them as in no other way. When the Arabic emplatic article AL is taken from this hard word *al*-chas-chischin, it is Chaschis-chin. The Assassins, were, also, called Druses or Druiseans. The learned author of the "Celtic Druids" states that he has *proved* these Druses to be both Druids and Culdees. In all accounts of the Assassins, they are said to have existed, in the East, in considerable numbers. They are, also, stated to have been found numerous by B. de Tudela not far from Samarcand or Balkh:—where he also describes many great tribes of what he calls *Jews* to live, *speaking the Chaldee language*, occupying the country, and possessing the government of it. He says that among these Jews are disciples of *the wise men.* He tells us that they occupy the mountains of *Haphton.* Here are, it is to be thought, the *Afghans*, and that too clearly to be disputed. Under the word Haphton lies hid the word Afghan, and the disciples of the *wise* man, Hakem, frequented the Temples of Solomon in Cashmere, etc., and were called Hakmites, Ishmaelians, and Battenians that is Buddheans. The word Hakem is nothing but the word HKN, which in the Chaldee means *wise.* All physicians, in the East, are called Hakem. All this goes to prove that not only did the Templars share doctrines with the Assassins and Ishmaelians, but that they were much older than the Crusades, and that the pretended origin of these people is totally false. The Gymnosophists, the Casideans, the Essenes, the Therapeuttae, the Dio-

nesians, the Eleusinians, the Pythagoreans, the
Chaldeans, the Assassins, and the Buddheans were
all an order of religionists, including among them,
and consisting in great part, an Order of Monks,
who were, in fact, the heads of the Society.

There is no doubt but that all the Caliphs of the
Saracens were, secretly or openly, Sophees. The
Sophees are divided, at this day, into many sects,
and, in their four stages, they have a species of
Masonic, or Eleusinian, initiation from lower to high-
er degrees, and this Order, it may be truthfully
said, has some of the greatest Mysteries in their
possession, now held by any Order or Fraternity
in the world at this day. Sir John Malcolm says,
Hassan Sabah, and his descendents, were a race of
Sophees, and that they were of the sect of Battan-
eah, that is Buddha. They were Templars, or
Casi-deans, or Chas-di-im, or followers of Ras or
Masons.

The use of the Pallium, or sacred cloak, to convey
the character of Inspiration, was practiced by the
Imaums of Persia, the same as practiced by Elias
and Elishah (Eli-shah). And it is continued by
their followers to this day. When a person is admitted to the highest degree, he will receive the investiture with the Pallium and the Samach. When
the Grand-Seignior means to honor a person, he
gives him a pellise, a Pall, a *pla*, a sacred cloak, a
remnant of the old superstition, the meaning probably being quite forgotten, From this comes the
word "palls" at our funerals.

One of the names, which excites the greatest

curiosity as to its meaning, of the chief of the Assassins, was "Old Man of the Mountain"—*senex de montibus*. The Buddwa of Scotland was called "old man;" and Buddha, in India, means *old man*. The opinion that the Assassins were Buddaists receives confirmation, in part, from the idea that he was reckoned as representative of the "ancient of days." The representative idea, or form, or figure by which the Prophet speaks of the Divine Intelligence— "Ancient of days," whose hair was wool, of a white color. But in Persian, according to Sir John Malcolm, the word *sofee* means both wisdom and wool. It is possible that from this idea we obtain the white goats' hair cloaks of the Albanians, with their "snowy *camese* and their shaggy *capote*;" the white bernoose of the Moors, the white robes of the Carmelites: even the white uniforms of the Austrian army—nay, the sacred acceptation, and the supposed enchanted value, of the color *white* generally.

That the renowned and dreadful tribes of Assassins, or Ishmaelites, whose history presents such an inextricable connection with that of the Templars, and also with that of the Hospitallers, were acquainted with, if not professors of the Fire-Creed of Zoroaster, (so little understood by the profane) from which, indeed, they derived their atheistic desperation, will be apparent when we examine their belief.

What was really the object of the worship of the Knights Templars, in their secret synods, none but the Initiate may know. Whether, indeed, in their intercourse with infidels, they had not imbibed

some of the ancient, traditionary ideas, and learned
the religion of the inhabitants of that part of Asia
bounded by Persia, on the one hand, and by the
Mediterranean on the other, seems a point more
readily settled in the affirmative. In this view,
Flame-worship would have passed a part of the
adopted rites. We are thus brought to contemplate the Templars not so much in the light of a
new superstition, as in *the brilliancy of the Philosophic position of the Magi* in the old world of thought,
and of the Rosicrucians, Brethren of the Rosy Cross,
or *illuminati*, in the new.

Lamps and cloisters, lamps and altars, lamps and
shrines, lights and tombs, lights (*fire*) everywhere,
are connected ideas. The romance lingering and
brightening about which strange subjects may have
its origin in the *real*, philosophic, unsuspected *truth*
which gives *life* to their meaning even for *all* time.
Romance *never* has life except for the truth which
underlies it. With these *Fires* among the graves—
with the ultimate and funeral burning—with the
pyre of the classics and the Fire-immolations of the
Orientals—with the *Sacred Fire* of the Magi, and the
cressets and the torches of the Christian Knightly
Fraternities, we connect the Ever-Burning lamps.
(always representing true Love and Immortality to
the Initiate but simply heathenism to the masses
and profane) of which we have archaeological
accounts, and the suspected, Ishmaelitish, Bohemi-
an or Fire-Worshipping Mysticism, which is nothing but Fire, or Love (God) worship, Harbored as
the "strange thing" among the cowles and stoles,

amidst the crosses and the books, and glancing, as the fiery crested snake (which is but a symbol of Love or Fire Wisdom) from among the resplendent arms of the supposed (by the profane) renegade Templars.

To this striking object of tomb-Lights—incoherent in any other view than as the attestation, through the ages, of a Universal, though a Secret Faith, Walter Scott accidentally (and unconsciously of its meaning) makes reference when he adjures the dying lamps as burning—

> "Before thy low and lonely urn,
> O gallant chief of Otter bourne;
> And thine, dark Knight of Liddesdale!"

Of the "grave of the mighty dead," Michael Scott, the wizard of such dreadful fame, he also says that, within it—

> "Burned a wonderous light;
> Which lamp shall burn unquenchably;"

which means the Soul, the Fire, the Love in man.

The only serious hold which it is possible to gain over the minds of men is through the influence of the supernatural.   It is absurd and inconsequential to believe that all the wonderful effects which the Templars and other Fraternities of Devotees, which seemed bound by a religion produced in their time, could have sprung from no higher motive than the desire to aggrandise—to overpower—to rule—to force. Wonderful things—unbelievable things— miraculous things---impossible things---must have been offered to the common-sense of the men of the age, before they would have given in to the authority which became to them as that of angels, of spirits, and of the gods. It is no slight task to master the resisting common-sense of the world. That which is invincible, except at conviction. Instincts at detection were as strong then as now. We are accustomed, every day, to the infallable judgements of common-sense. That decision as to what a thing is, is as independent of us as the sense of light. Quick wit, sharp wits, hardness of unbelief, suspicion, the same reason as is at work now---these were identical in the dark ages---in any age that man was man. Prophecy must have been wonderfully verified---the assumed magic must have been demonstrated real---something not at all a fraud---first, before imaginative and enthusiastic men, themselves, could believe it; second, before plain men could accept that which sense assured was impossible.

There existed in those secret societies, the dreams, trances, visions, magic-spells, magic-sight, which made princes of the Seers. It is in this secret medium---whatever it may be---whether conjured out of the capacity of man in the intoxication of narcotics, through fumes, anointings, training, or lapsing out of the prisoned sense into the unimprisoned sense:---it is in their new world that the explorers stumble upon unbelievable, though real, things. Of a piece with the miraculous prevision obtained by the Grand Master of the Templars, in his agony, as noticed hereafter, was the following two instances of forecasting, which, as far as can

14

be affirmed by records, are definitely established. The Priestess Phoennis, the daughter of a Chaonic King, foretold the devastating march of the Gauls, and the course which they would take from Europe to Asia, together with the destruction of the cities, and this a generation before the event happened. The King Phrrhus had received an oracular sentence---that he was destined to die as soon as he had seen a wolf fighting with a bull. The sentence was fulfilled when in the market-place of Argos, he saw a bronze group representing such a combat. An old woman killed him by throwing down a tile from a house.

The Assassins, as a secret sect, had a kind of University among them. The course of instruction in this university proceeded, according to Macrisi, by the following nine degrees.

The object of the first section of instruction, which was long and tedious, was to infuse doubts and difficulties into the minds of the aspirant, and to lead him to repose, with a blind, admiring confidence, in the knowledge and wisdom of the teachers. To this end he was perplexed with extraordinary, and seemingly unanswerable, questions. The absurdities of the literal sense of the Koran, and its repugnance to reason, were studiously pointed out. Dark hints were given that, beneath the shell of the philosophy taught, lay a kernel sweet to the taste and nutritive to the soul. But all further information was most rigorously withheld from the inquiring mind until the disciple had consented to bind himself, by a most solemn oath, to absolute faith and obedience to his instructor.

In the second place, when the aspirant had taken the prescribed oath, he was admitted as a member of the second degree, in which was inculcated the acknowledgement of the particulars appointed by God as the sources of all knowledge. This included science, and the arts and truths of life.

The third degree included the knowledge of farther important facts, and the connection, and succession, and power of those facts. It also informed the student what was the number of the blessed and holy *imams*. And this was the mystic seven; for as God hath made seven heavens, seven earths, seas, planets, metals, tones, and colors, so seven was the number of the noblest angels, spirits, or attributes of God. Religion, as yet, was not outstept.

In the fourth degree, the pupil learned that God had sent *seven* lawgivers into the world, each of whom was commissioned to alter and improve, or rather to develop, the system of his predecessor; that each of these had seven helpers, who appeared in the interval between him and his successor; these helpers, as they did not appear as public teachers, were called the mute (*samit*), in contradistinction to the *speaking* lawgivers. The seven lawgivers were Adam, Noah, Abraham, Moses, Jesus, Mohammed, and Ismail, the son of Jaaffer; the seven principal helpers, called Seats (Soos), were Seth, Shem, Ismael the son of Abraham, Aaron, Simon, Ali, and Mohammed, the son of Ismail. It is justly observed by the discerning Hammer that, as this last personage was not more than a century dead, the teacher had it in his power to fix on whom he would as the mute prophet of the present time, and inculcate the belief in, and obedience to, him of all who had not got beyond this degree.

The fifth degree taught that each of the seven mute prophets had twelve apostles for the dissemination of his faith. The suitableness of this number also proved by analogy. There are twelve signs of the Zodiac, twelve months, twelve tribes of Israel, twelve joints in the four fingers of each hand, and so forth. This all proves that this school was founded on facts that were absolute and not to be contradicted then or at the present time.

In the sixth place, the disciple being carefully led thus far, and his mind being duly prepared for what followed, the Koran, and the precepts contained in that book of authority, were once more brought under consideration, and he was told that all the positive portions of religion, and all the facts of faith, must be subordinated to the laws of nature and reconciled to the lights of philosophy, or be rejected as perhaps necessary to the apprehension, though intrinsically worthless. In fact, man herein was thrown back upon nature, and taught to discover the exterior influences alone in it. Then succeeded, for a long space of time, instruction in the systems of Plato and Aristotle. When esteemed fully qualified, the scholar was admitted to the seventh degree, in which knowledge was imparted in that mystic Pantheism which is held and taught by the sect of the Sofees. This was Buddhism, without the supernatural light of Bhuddism.

As an eighth step into the *arcana* of philosophy, the positive doctrine of religion were considered in their light as a *necessity* to man, and as resulting from his position here in this world.   All the complicated knowledge which had now preceded was declared, in the forward stage of the student's progress, to be merely as the scaffolding by which the piling of the structure of real knowledge was to be effected.   All the builder's platforms and his poles, his work being now complete, were to be thrown down.   Prophets and teachers, heaven and hell, all the shows of life, its history, the machinery of the world, the human soul, were nothing.   Future bliss and future misery, reckoning for evil, conscience beyond the necessity of the maintenance of regularity in the world, aspiration for good out of the pleasant things of the world, justice and moderation beyond that common-sense of economy for the longer lasting, the intrinsic value of life, and the detriment from the destruction of it other than in the policy of a certain blank atheistic "political economy"—all these were to be exposed as idle dreams, having nothing to do with the philosopher, whose sight had been cleared by a magic illumination, darkening or eclipsing, or overpowering, or *putting out* the false light of the world.   Even as the light of day is drawn over the stars like a curtain.

In this absolute laying-level of the barriers of right and wrong, the point of view became consistent as showing that all actions should proceed, alone, from the center point of self-pleasure in them, that power was right and that right was power, and that all laws were imported only into the world as

14 I

securing the harmonious going on of it. That, in
the absolute sense, there could be no such thing as
sin; that therefore, in the absolute sense, there
could be no such thing as punishment for it. Therefore, that nothing was to be feared on the score of
conscience. Life was as a weed.

The ninth and last degree was that into which
the disciple transcended (in this alarming sense),
as seeing that, as nothing was to be believed, everything might be done.

Von Hammer argues an identity between the two
orders, as he styles them, of the Ishmaelites and
the Templars from the similarity of their dress,
their internal organization, and their secret doctrine. The color of the Khalifs of the house of
Ommiyah was white; hence the house of Abbas, in
their contest with them, adopted black as their dis-
tinguishing hue. Hassan Sabah, when he formed
the institution of the *fedavee*, or the "Devoted to
Death," assigned them a red girdle or cap. The
mantle worn by the members of the Hospital was
black.

The last Grand Master of the Templars, Jacques
de Molay, together with his companion, Guy,
brother to the Dauphin of Auvergne, were brought
forth and placed upon a pile erected upon that point
of the islet of the Seine, at Paris, where afterwards
was erected the statue of Henry IV. It was a day
of March—the 19th, as it is stated by the historians
—1314. The two unfortunate Templars suffered
with constancy, to the last asserting their inno-
cence. The spectators wept and shrieked at the

spectacle of their sacrifice. During the night their ashes were gathered up to be preserved as relics.

Molay, ere he expired, summoned Clement, the Pope who had pronounced the bull of abolition against the Order and had condemned the Grand Master to the flames, to appear, within forty days, before the Supreme Eternal Judge, and Phillip to the same awful but just tribunal within the space of a year.   Both predictions were fullfilled and thus was justice meted out. The Pontiff did actually die of a colic on the night of the 19th of the following month. More dreadful still, the church in which his body was deposited in state, took fire, the flames spread, and the corpse of Clement was half consum- ed. The King, before the year had elapsed, by an accidental fall from his horse, suffered such injury, that he, also, died. The fullfillment of these two prophecies showed to what extent the Masters of the Order had developed and produced great effect. The unfortunate Templars were justly regarded as Matyrs.

We know that the general—nay, the universal be- lief is to the contrary—but that the Order of the Knights Templars, in certain forms, has continued down to the present day. The King of Portugal, in his dominions, formed the Order of Christ out of the Templars. The Freemasons also were connected with the ancient Templars; and there is a society, bearing the name of Brethren of the Temple, whose chief seat is at Paris, and its branches extend into various countries, and into England. Jacques de Molay, in the year 1814, in anticipation of his speedy matyrdom, appointed Johannes Marcus Lormenius to be his successor in his dignity, and there has been an unbroken, though secret, succession of Grand Masters down to the present time.   The secret doctrines of the Templars were partaken of by the Knights of the Order of St John of Jerusalem we also have proof of.   Signor Rossetti, who possessed a very intimate acquaintance with the history of the Hospitallers, maintains stoutly that there is much in common between the doctrines taught in the higher grades of the Freemasons—more, also, that has been lost—and the views, *formulae*, and fashions of the Order of the Temple.   True Masons, who know the *spirit* of their Fraternity as well as the rituals, *know* that Masonry sprung from the Templars.

Lost in the clouds of antiquity, the dim forms of the mailed Templars disappear.   Their buildings, their churches, their haunts remain.   But the inhabitants are passed into the shadows.   Their remembrances and their secrets only survive in the quaint courts of the Temples.   The fact that their dwelling-place was once within the present purlieus of law—that the notes of their wild Eastern music, and that the ceremonies of their strange, deeply Occult worship, were in the time that has almost become a dream, real matters in the story of those, at present, so unromantic buildings—truths amidst this wilderness of mechanical-law-spelling:—these things of a life, so unlike our present life, lend an interest to the very name of the Temples yet standing, holding their secrets as ever and defying the crude and unnatural investigations of the profane but so well-known to the true Initiate.

There exist real personal memorials of this antique and wonderful body of the Templars preserved, in secret at the present time, in Paris. Some of the archives and statutes—portions of the unexamined history—even some of the mystic banners, and an assortment of the arms of the brotherhood; still survive. These are kept in unknown but *not* in obscure or dilapidated buildings as some, for want of knowledge, seem to think. Strange that the world should think that the secrets of such a mighty sect of Fire Philosophers, once living, should ever die. Such things cannot be. God does not allow it to be.

The Therapeutae and Essenes and Their Initiation

THE Order of the Essenes constituted in the time of Jesus the final remnant of those Brotherhoods of prophets organized by Samuel. The despotism of the rulers of Palestine, the jealousy of an ambitious and servile priesthood, had forced them to take refuge in silence and solitude. They no longer struggled as did their predecessors, but contented themselves with preserving their traditions. They had two principal centres, one in Egypt, on the banks of Lake Maoris, the other in Palestine, at Engaddi, near the Dead Sea. The names of the Essenes they had adopted came from the Syrian word assaya, a physician — in Greek, therapeutis; for their only acknowledged ministry with regard to the public was that of healing disease both physical and moral. They studied with great diligence certain medical writings dealing with the occult virtue of plants and mineral.

It is on account of the Syrian word "Assaya," that the mistake is made in regard to the Essenes and Therapeutæ. The Therapeutæ was only a branch of the Essenes with but different duties.

The branch known as the Therapeutæ had their home chiefly on the Lake Mareotis, near Alexandria, but also had colonies in other places. Like the parent Order—the Essenes, they lived unmarried, in monasteries, and were very moderate with regard to dress and food; they prayed at sunrise having their faces turned to the East; studied the Secret Doctrine and Greater Mysteries of Antiquity. They differed from the Essenes in that they lived a contemplative life, while the Essenes followed many occupations, such as agriculture, arts, sciences, etc. The Essenes lived together in common; the Therapeutæ lived separately and alone. The Therapeutæ, being of the Outer Degree, knew none of the divisions which marked the several degrees of Initiation of the Inner Circle—the Essenes. Both Orders resembles the Pythagoreans and the teachings were identical. Neither used animal food, and both the Inner and the Outer admitted women to their assemblies and Initiation.

The Essenes, living a more active life, bore a very important, though secret part in the development of Judaism. John the Baptist belonged to their ranks before Christ was admitted.

Some of them possessed the gift of prophecy, as, Menahim, who had prophesied to Herod that he should reign. They served God with great piety, not by offering victims but by sanctifying the spirit; avoiding towns, they devoted themselves to the arts of peace; not a single slave was found to be among them; they were all free and worked for one another. The rules of the Order were very strict as was necessary in such times. In order to enter, a year's novitiate was necessary. If one had given sufficient proofs of temperance, he was admitted to the ablutions, though without entering into relations with the Masters of the Order. Tests, extending over another

two years, were necessary before being received into
the Brotherhood. They swore "by terrible oaths" to
observe the rules of the Order and to betray none of
its secrets. Then only did they participate in the
common repasts, which were celebrated with great
solemnity and constituted the Inner worship of the
Essenes. The garments they had worn during these
repasts they looked upon as sacred and to be removed before resuming work. These fraternal Love-
feasts, primitive form of the Supper instituted by
Jesus,* began and ended by prayer. The first interpretation of the sacred books of Moses and the prophets was here given. But the explanation of the texts
allowed of three significations. All this wonderfullly
resembled the organization of the Pythagoreans, but
it was almost the same amongst all the ancient
prophets, for *it is the same wherever true initiation
has ever existed.* The Essenes professed the essential
dogma of the Orphic and Pythagorean doctrine; that
of the pre-existence of the soul, the consequence and
reason of its Immortality. The soul descending from
the most subtle ether, and attracted into the body by
a certain natural charm, remains there as in a prison;
freed from the bonds of the body, as from a long
servitude, it joyfully takes its flight.

Among the Essenes, as has been stated, the brothers, properly so called, lived under a community of

---

* This Love-feast is kept up by many of the churches, especially those known as the "Dunkards," "Methodists," but
what a mockery it is. The Essenes and the Christ never even
tasted meat, much less used it at the Love-feast, but these
churches must have their Roasted meats in order to have the
Love-feast of the Christ. Blood! blood must be everywhere.

property, and in a condition of celibacy, cultivating the ground, and, at times, educating the children of strangers. The married Essenes, for there were such, formed a class affiliated and under subjection to the other. Silent, gentle, and grave, they were to be met with here and there, cultivating the Arts of Peace. Carpenters, weavers, vine-planters, or gardeners, never gunsmiths or merchants. Scattered in small groups about the whole of Palestine, and in Egypt, even as far as Mount Horeb, they offered one another the most complete hospitality. Thus we see Jesus and his disciples journeying from town to town, and from province to province, and always certain of finding shelter and lodging. Thus it is ever with the *true* Initiate. "Do unto others as you would that they should do unto you."

The Essenes, as all true Initiates, were of an exemplary morality, they forced themselves to suppress passion and anger; *transmuting* it into Love. Always benevolent, peaceable, and trustworthy. Their word was more powerful than an oath, which, in ordinary life, they looked upon as superfluous, and almost a perjury. They endured the most cruel of tortures, with admirable steadfastness of soul and smiling countenance rather than violate the slightest religious precept. Indifferent to the outward pomp of worship at Jerusalem, repelled by the harshness of the Sadducees, and the prayers of the Pharisees, as well as by the pedantry of the synagogue, Jesus was attracted towards the Essenes by natural affinity.

From the Essenes, Jesus received what they alone could give him: the Esoteric tradition of the proph-

ets, and by its means, his own historical and religious tendency or trend.   He was taught how wide
was the gulf that separated the official Jewish doctrine from the Ancient Wisdom of the Initiates, the
veritable mother of religions, though ever persecuted by Satan—by the spirit of evil, of egotism, hatred
and denial, allied with absolute political power and
priestly imposture.   He learned that Genesis, under
the seal of its symbolism, concealed a theogony and
cosmogony as far removed from their literal signification as is the profoundest truth of science from
a child's fable.   He contemplated the days of Aelo-
him, or the eternal creation by emanation of the
elements and the formation of the worlds, the origin
of the floating souls, and their return to God by progressive existences or generations of Adam.   He was
taught the grandeur of the thoughts of Moses, whose
intention had been to prepare the religious unity of
the nations by establishing the worship of the one
God, and incarnating this idea into a people.

He was instructed in the doctrine of the divine
Word, *already taught by Krishna in India, by the
priests of Osiris, by Orpheus and Pythagoras in
Greece, and known to the prophets under the name
of The Mysteries of the Son of Man and of the Son
of God.*   According to this doctrine, the highest manifestation of God is man, who, in constitution, form,
organs and intelligence is the image of the Universal
Being, whose faculties he possesses.   In the earthly
evolution of humanity, however, God is scattered,
split up, and mutilated, so to speak, in the multipli-
city of men and of the human imperfections.   In it
he struggles, suffers, and tries to find himself, he is

the Son of Man, the Perfect Man, the Man–Type,
the profoundest thought of God, remaining hidden
in the infinite abyss of his desire and power. At
certain epochs, when humanity is to be saved from
some terrible gulf, and set on a higher stand, a chos-
en one identifies himself with divinity, attracts it to
himself by strength, wisdom, and love, and mani-
fects it anew to men. Then, divinity, by the virtue
and breath of the Spirit, is completely present in
him: the Son of Man becomes the Son of God, and
his Living Word. In other ages and among other
nations, there had already appeared sons of God,
but since Moses, none had arisen in Israel. All the
prophets were expecting this Messiah. The Seers
even said that this time he would call himself the
Son of Woman, of the Heavenly Isis, of the divine
light which is the Bride of God, for the light of
Love would shine in him.

All these secrets which the patriarch of the Essenes unfolded to the young Galilean on the solitary
banks of the Dead Sea, in lonely Engaddi, seemed to
him wonderful, but yet known. It was with no ordinary emotion that he heard the chief of the Order
comment on the words still to be read in the Book
of Henoch: "From the beginning the Son of Man was
in the Mystery. The Father kept him near his
mighty presence, and *manifested him to his elect.*
But the Kings shall be afraid and shall prostrate
themselves to the ground with terror, when they shall
see the *Son of Woman* seated on the throne of his
glory. Then the elect shall summon all the forces
of heaven, all the saints from on high and the power
of God; and the Cherubim, the Seraphim, the Opha-

nim, all the angels of *Might,* all the angels of the *Lord, i. e.,* of the Elect, and *of the other Might,* serving on earth and above the waters, shall raise their voices."

I have thought best to give this much concerning the Essenes and their teachings in order to make plain what the Essenes were. Very little is known of them in the Christian church although the Master—Christ was of them. The church even denies that Christ was an Initiate and disbelieves that such a thing as Initiation exists. It is strange that this should be so and no one is to be thanked more for this state than Constantine.

A history of the Philosophers would not be complete without dwelling on the Essenian Order for the reason that the Ancient Mysteries took another form after the Initiation of Christ. Their teachings are therefore of vital importance and show that the Essenian Fraternity knew the teachings of *all* other Orders or religious beliefs and that it was but a continuation of previous Orders under another name. And what of the teachings concerning Initiation? In secret records we find the following:

"The union of God with the soul is the principle of all Mystic life. But this union, the fulness and final consummation of which cannot be experienced till death has been passed through and eternity has been achieved, can be accomplished on this earth in a more or less perfect manner, and the literature of entire Mysticism has no other end than to unveil to us. by a full and profound analysis of the different stages of evolution in the spirit of man, the diverse successive degrees of this Divine union. Seven dis-

tinct stages of the soul's ascent towards God have
been recognized by Mystics, and they constitute what
has been emblematically called the Castle of the Interior man.   They represent the seven absolute processes of psychic transfiguration.   The first link in
this Arcane sequence is called the state of prayer,
which, from the pneumatic standpoint, is the concentration of the intellectual energies upon God as
the object of thought, which is commonly assisted
by the ceremonial appeal made by religion of the
senses.   It has, however, a higher aspect, comprised
in the second evolutionary process, and called the
state of mental prayer.   Here the illusionary phenomena of the visible world, are regarded as informed
with the Inner pneumatic significance, to divine
which is a chief end of Mysticism.   In order to make
progress therein, and so attain the third stage, it is
necessary that the Aspirant, shaping all practical
life in conformity with this theory, should perform
no outward act except with a view to its inward
meaning, all things which are of time and earth, and
man being simply figures and symbols of earth and
heaven and God.   The postulant as he advances will
perceive that the inmost thoughts of his own conscience being are only a limited and individual speculation of the speech or word of God, concealed even
in its apparent relevation, and itself a veil of the
Divine truth which must be removed for the contemplation of the truth absolute, which is behind it.
When he has reached this point the Mystic will have
entered on the third stage of his illumination. This
is the most difficult of all.   It is termed by Mystics
the obscure night, and here it is necessary that the

aspirant should become stark naked,—*should empty himself completely, should be stripped of all his faculties, renouncing all his own predilictions, his own thoughts, his own will—in a word, his whole self.* Aridity, weariness, temptation, desolation, darkness, are characteristic of this epoch, (see Initiation of Christ), and they have been experiences by all who have ever made any progress in the Mysteries of Mystical Love. The fourth condition is denominated the prayer of quietism. Complete immolation of self and unreserved surrender into the hands of God, have respose as their first result. Such quietism, however, is not to be confounded with insensibility, for it leads to the soul real activity, to that which has God for its impulse. The fifth degree in the successive spiritualization of the human soul is called the state of union, in which the will of man and the will of God become substantially identified. This is Mystical irrigation which fertilizes the garden of the Soul. During this portion of his development, the Neophyte, imbued with a sovereign disdain of all things visible, as well as for himself, accomplishes in peace, serenity, and joy of spirit, the will of God supernaturally speaking *within* him. On the extreme further limit of this condition, the Mystic enters the sixth state, which is that of ecstatic prayer, which is the soul's transport above and outside itself. It constitutes a union with Divinity by the instrument of positive love which is a state of Sanctification, beatitude, and ineffable torrents of delight flowing over the whole being. It is beyond description, it transcends illustration, and its felicity is not to be conceived. *Love* which is a potency of the soul,

or of the anima which vivifies our bodies, has passed
into the spirit of the soul, into its superior, divine,
and universal form, and this process completed com-
prises the seventh and final state of pneumatic development, which is that of ravishment.   Renouncing all that is corporeal about it, the soul becomes a
pure spirit, capable of being united, in a wholly celestial manner to the Uncreated Spirit, whom it beholds, loves, serves, adores above and beyond all
created forms, and this is the Mystic marriage,* the
perfect union, and entrance of God and Heaven into
the interior of man.

We have thus the teachings of the Essenes which
show that they were but a continuation of the Secret
Doctrine and Mysteries of Antiquity.   It proves that
true Initiation is to-day as it was in the time of the
Christ.   Since then, the Mysteries are better known
as the Christian Mysteries.   They are all the same
and will ever continue to be the same.   Truth never
changes and no matter under what name, or by what
Order these Mysteries may be taught they are the
same as were taught at Atlantis and by all the great
Saviours since then.   In order to more fully understand this Initiation of man into the Mysteries, we
will need to understand the Initiation of Christ by
the Essenes, more fully and as we find them given
to us in "The Life of Jehoshua (Jesus), the Prophet
of Nazareth," by Dr. Hartmann.

"After Jesus had entered the Essenian temple, he
was led into the presence of the assembled priests.
They questioned him in regard to his object in de-

---

* See "The Chymical Marriage of Christian Rosencreutz."

siring to enter their Order, and admonished him to
desist; warning him of the dangers that he would
incur, if he insisted in pursuing his way to obtain
knowledge of the Secret Science and to come in possession of the powers which such knowledge conveyed. They told him that if he were once admitted,
*there could be no possibility to retreat, as he would
have to succeed or lose his freedom and perhaps even
his life; for powers of evil which would be aroused
would conquer him, unless he were strong enough to
conquer them.*

Jesus was not to be intimidated; he desired to
obtain knowledge and considered wisdom to be *more*
valuable than life. He insisted upon being admitted.
He received the blessings of the Brothers, and as
each of these venerable men laid his hand upon his
head, he felt an electric thrill pass through his frame,
that seemed to invigorate him and to give him a
power sufficient to overcome all dangers. After this
he was given over to a guide called *Thesmophores,*
who blindfolded him and led him away.

He went with his guide through several long cor-
ridors, from whose walls the echoes of their steps resounded, and they descended a flight of stairs until
at last they arrived at the place of their destination.
When the hood was removed, Jesus found himself in
a cave hewn in the solid rock. It was a high arched
vault with massive pillars, cut in a manner to represent figures of men and fabulous animals. The only
light which entered into the vault came through a
round opening far up in the roof, where a small part
of the clear sky could be seen. Upon the walls of
that prison were written proverbs and mottoes, con-

15 I

sisting of extracts from the books of the Egyptian
and Indian sages who may have lived in the far-distant past, perhaps even in prehistoric times, when
that which we now call Europe formed the bottom of
the sea, and another continent—Beautiful and
Glorious Atlantis—was at the height of its civilization at a place where now the ocean rolls its waves.

The room was furnished in the most primitive
fashion, containing merely the most necessary requis-
ites. The Thesmophores told the Neophyte—for
such Jesus had become—that he would have to remain here in solitude for an indefinite period of
time. He advised him to occupy himself with thinking of the nature of man and his destiny and to
meditate about his own self.—"Man, Know Thyself." He gave him some writing material and re-
quested him to write down the thoughts that would
enter his mind and seem important to him, and after
taking leave of the prisoner and wishing him good
success, the guide went away.

*Thus when the free spirit seeking for knowledge
sends its feelers into the tomb of living clay, blindly
following the Law of Reincarnation, he finds himself alone without a guide, left to his own thoughts,
and with only a faint light above coming from his
former home, while on the walls of the prison house
called the Mind, he finds dim recollections of the
teachings of wisdom acquired in previous lives.*

*Jesus was now alone. There is nothing more ter-
rible than isolation and solitude to those who know of
no other life but that of external sensation and who
cannot create their own thoughts; especially if there
is no change in their surroundings, to attract their*

*attention and to stimulate them to think. Thinking
is an Art, and few can think what they wish or hold
on to a thought. Men only think what they must;
they feed on the ideas that enter their minds without
asking. Welcome and unwelcome thoughts enter;
they neither come at our bidding nor go away when
they are not wanted; they are like disorderly guests
that do not obey the rules which the landlord pre-
scribes.*

The monotony in which Jesus lived remained un-
changed.   There was no sound of any kind to be
heard; he was surrounded by silence; and if it had
not been for the small opening in the vault far above
his head, he would not have known the change of
day and night.   He studied the writings upon the
walls, and impressed them upon his memory, analyz-
ing their meaning; and the more he thought about
them, the more his mind seemed to expand and new
ideas entered.   He could not tell from when they
came, but he wrote them down upon the tablets with
which he had been supplied; and often when in the
morning he awoke from his slumber, these tablets
had disappeared from his prison, and he knew not
what had become of them.   He saw no one enter the
room, and yet somebody must have taken them away.
Likewise the food with which he was provided was
supplied by invisible hands.   It was of the most
simple kind, consisting of bread, milk, fruit, and
water.   It was daily brought to him in some inex-
plicable manner; how or by what means he could not
tell, for it was put into his prison during his sleep.
However, he soon ceased to be astonished at such
strange occurrences and he began seriously the study

of self. As he became accustomed to look *within* his own soul, a new world semed to open before him; his imagination grew stronger, and the pictures presented before his *inner* eye became as objective and real to him as the objects of the external world, only . more beautiful, more ethereal, and yet far more substantial than the latter. Visions of things which he had formerly seen, but which had apparently been lost to his memory, appeared again, vivid and real with all their living details; desires entering his heart immediately took objective forms in his mind, representing in seemingly living forms the objects of which he thought, and thus he saw many beautiful things in his visions, but also many horrible sights, for no man is without evil, and evil thoughts that came to him were likewise represented in seemingly real but horrible form.

What is this plastic power of the imagination, and what do men mean by calling subjective images *"merely* works of imagination?" Can we imagine anything that does not exist? Are the creations of our thoughts less real to us than the things which the imagination of others created for us for all things must exist first in the imagination? Is not the universe itself a product of the imagination of God, and are we not gods in our own Inner world, able to create forms from the substance called the *astral light?*

Gradually Jesus began to love this *inner* life, where he found a world as large as the outer world, with a space as infinite as that of the latter, with mountains and plains, with oceans and rivers, and peopled with beings of various kinds that looked up to him as their god, their creator, drawing life from his Will, and nourishment from his Thoughts, in the same sense as Man receives his will-power and ideas from the God in the universe, appearing to him in his dreams while asleep, and in visions while awake. Thus Jesus lived in the world of the *Elemental Powers* of Nature, and began to know the constituent parts of that organism called the human soul.

Weeks, perhaps months, thus passed away. We cannot say how long he remained in that tomb. He kept no record of the days and nights since he had entered there, and what is time and space, after all, but merely mental conceptions by which we attempt to measure the Infinite? But one day steps were heard to approach, and the Thesmophores entered, congratulating him on his success and inviting him to come to the Portal of Man, to enter as a Neophyte into the first degree of the Holy Brotherhood.

They entered a large park, through which they passed, until they arrived at an entrance called the *Door of the Profane.* There they found a great many people assembled who had been attracted by curiosity to see the new candidate for initiation, for such a rare event was not kept secret as it was desired thatt he people should know that there were still men to be found ready to dare all dangers in search of the truth. They thronged the place in front of the door through which Jesus passed with his guide, on his way to the Temple of Wisdom; they shouted and made much noise, obstructing the way; but the Thesmophores drove them back, and they passed safely through the crowd. (This must not be understood in its literal sense. The people that had been assembled and who made noise and obstructed the way, must be understood as the lower Elementals that have their being in all men until they are overcome by Light and Love. This is also the meaning of Transmuting the Baser, or lower, metals into the pure gold, or Higher nature).

Having entered the vestibule of the temple, the candidate was taken to a Crypt, where he took a bath (became purified), and received new garments, and underwent the prescribed preparation to be introduced to the assembly of Brothers.

The *Portal of Man* was guarded by the *Pastophores,* who, as they arrived, inquired about their purpose and asked Jesus various questions. Having received satisfactory replies, the door opened, and he entered a large hall, wherein in a semicircle were seated the Brothers, and in their midst the *Hierophant.* Before this assembly Jesus again passed an examination, answering numerous questions in regard to his subjective experiences during his isolation. (The student will easily comprehend that it is from this part of Christ's Initiation that the story of his being in the Temple before the Priests, took form. Christ was certainly before the Priests, and astonised them by his apt answers to their questions, but the Bible story is but a legend founded on truth as are all legends, no matter how untruthful they may seem.)

He was then led around the *Bisantha,* and there the strength of his nerves and his physical courage, by certain methods which cannot be made intelligible to the modern reader, because they involve an employment of certain forces of nature, the secret of which was in the possession of the *Atlanteans* and *Egyptians*, but whose very existence is as yet unknown to western civilization. It may be sufficient to say, that if claps of thunder resounded and bolts of lightning seemed to strike the candidate, they were not produced in the manner employed in theatrical performances upon the stage, but they were the effects of natural forces, set into action by the occult powers possessed by the Egyptian Adepts. The most horrible spectres appeared, but Jesus was not afraid.

Having successfully passed through this trial, he was again taken before the assembly, and the *Menis* read to him the laws of the *Crata Repoa*, which after due examination, he solemnly promised to obey. By a certain process known to the Hierophant, his spiritual vision was then opened; that is to say, he was endowed for a short time with the powers to see certain spiritual verities represented in allegorical forms. He found himself standing between *two square columns*, called *Bestiles*, and there was a *ladder with seven steps* and *eight closed doors—the external senses.* As he beheld that vision, its meaning was at once clear to him, for spiritual visions differ from mere dreams especially in so far as he who beholds a symbolical vision becomes at the same time aware of its meaning, else it would be useless to show such a vision to him. *No vision is possible, nor will the spiritual sight be opened to the initiate unless he first has learned, through long training and concentration, to silence the senses and passions of the moral frame.* In that short moment, during which his inner sight was opened, Jesus learned to know the fundamental principles of the Cosmos, a science which would require many months of instruction to be described in words and to be brought to the understanding of the not self-luminous intellect. *Knowledge cannot be gained by any outside teachings. We can take a teacher's authority for what he may tell us, but we cannot know, or have knowledge unless the inner perceptions, the very soul, tells us that it is so and given the wherefore. From the inner being— the spirit, alone can come knowledge and understanding.*

The Hierophant then spoke as follows: "I am speaking only to you who have the right and the power to hear me—*the materialist has neither right nor power to know inner truths, it is only he, who through training and right living, has been enabled to awaken the still small voice, the inner being, who can understand spiritual truths.* Firmly close all the doors—*external senses*—and exclude all the profane, the sophists and scoffers—*prejudices;* but you, children of the celestial labor—*spiritual perception,* hear my words: Beware of passions and evil desires; beware of erroneous opinions and intellectual prejudices. Keep your mind continually directed toward the divine source of all existence, strive after a continual realization of the presence of the Supreme; and if you desire to walk upon the Path of Light to Eternal happiness, do not forget for even a moment, that you are living in the consciousness of Him whose power has created the world. He is all things and all things are in Him. He is self-existent, pure knowledge, pure wisdom; and although He is seen by no man, there is nothing within the Universe that can hide itself from His sight."

Jesus had now become a member of the Brother-hood. *He was taught the laws of Nature, and made to see there is nothing dead in Nature, but that all forms are manifestations of the one Universal power of Life. He was taught the cause of the physical phenomena occurring in the world of phenomena, the nature of Light and Sound, of Heat and Electricity, and all other things. He was also instructed in Astronomy and Medicine and in the science of Hieroglyphics.*

The spiritual nature of Man was explained to him and the laws of Reincarnation. How the human monad again and again descends to build up a mortal physical form and to evolve a new personality at each of its visits upon this globe; that the human form, which we know as men, women and children, are not the real Man, but merely ever-changing aggregations of matter, endowed with an ever-changing consciousness, unsubstantial although living illusions, doomed to perish when the Spirit retires to its home, to rest from its labor; while the substantial, indivisible, and incorruptible Spirit is the real Man, although invisible to the perception of mortals.

He was taught the signification of the sacred syllable aum and of certain symbolical signs, including the double-interlaced Triangle, the Snake, and the Tam, and his office was to guard the portals of man, so that nothing impure would enter; for no one was ever admitted into the sanctuary of the Inner temple, unless he first proved himself a faithful guardian of

*that door by which evil thoughts and desires attempt
to enter the mind.*

A year or more may have passed by, when the *new*
Pastophores obtained permission to enter the second
degree, called *Necoris*. As a preparation for this
degree he had to undergo a severe fasting, after which
he was introduced into a grotto, called *Endymion*.

This grotto was furnished in a luxuriant manner.
It was without windows, but lamps that were suspended from the ceiling, and fed with perfumed oil,
shed a soft light through the room. The richest
food and the most delicious wines were set before
the Neophyte, and he was invited to partake; for now
—so they told him—he had won the victory, and he
might now indulge in sensual pleasures without any
risk of sin. The most beautiful maidens waited on
him, and their bewitching smiles told him that he
had only to mention a wish, to see it fulfilled. It
was evident that he was an object of admiration to
them, and that they were willing to be his slaves.

But Jesus resisted their *tempting* wiles. His *aspirations were for something far higher than the grati-
fication of sensual appetites;* the beauty of the corporeal form, however pleasing it may be to the eyes,
could not enslave him who *has learned to know the
beauty of the Spirit,* and as the evening approached,
the fair *tempters,* with looks full of disappointment
and unfulfilled desire, disappeared one after another,
and Jesus, after securely locking the door, threw
himself upon a couch.

While he was meditating there, a slight noise attracted his attention, and he saw one of the most
beautiful females that mortal eye ever beheld, en-

tering through a secret door, whose existence had escaped his observation. She was of most noble appearance and stately form, clad in loose, flowing garments, and with a sparkling diadem upon her head. Thus may have looked the chaste goddess Diana, when she watched the sleeping Endymion. An expression full of pity and love rested upon her face, as she approached the couch where Jesus rested.

"Fear nothing," she said; "I do not come to tempt but to save thee. I am the daughter of the guardian of this temple, and I have learned the danger which is threatening thee. Dost thou not know that these villainous priests have resolved to kill thee? for thou hast forfeited thy life by learning some of their mysteries. Thou, a foreigner, hast learned secrets which no one but the Egyptians are permitted to know. This evening they have resolved to kill thee, and the murder is to be executed even to-night. I have come to save thee; I have made sure thy escape; rise and follow me, for I admire thy valor and I do not wish thee to perish."

"Beautiful one," answered Jesus, "I will not dispute they words; but if the priests have resolved to kill me, let them do so; *for I have promised to obey the laws of this brotherhood, and I have no right to escape.*"

"Is there not," answered the *temptress*, "a higher law than the laws made by these priests? Is there not the law of nature, superior to all other laws? Does not the law of they nature permit and command thee to save thyself?"

"Spare thy words," answered Jesus. *"I know my*

duty. I shall remain and await whatever my fate may be."

"Then," said the lady, "I must tell thee what my modesty forbids me to say. It is not the life of a fugitive that I came to offer to thee, but a life of un- bounded love, a life of happiness and of luxury. Yes," she continued after a pause, drawing still near- er to him and putting her soft white hand upon his shoulder, "I love thee. Look into my eyes and see whether or not what I am telling is true. Wilt thou bury thy manhood in these living tombs, to seek after things which exist merely in thy imagination? Come with me, and I will give thee a substantial happiness far superior to any that thou mayst find within these gloomy walls. Can there be any great- er happiness for a man than the love of a beautiful woman? I. am rich, I am free, I am beautiful; I love thee with all the passionate love of which woman is capable. Come with me, and thou shalt never repent it."

"Fair one," answered Jesus, "all the earthly ele- ments of my *material* nature are striving to fly to thy embrace; but they are held by the *superior* will of the *spirit*. I do not seek for happiness within these walls, nor could I find contentment in the things which thou offerest me. I seek for happiness in that which is not subject to change; that which thou canst give is subject to decay. I reject thy offer."

"Dare to reject it!" answered the woman. "Dost thou know what a woman whose love is spurned can do? I shall not leave thee, for my soul clings to thee; to be separated from thee would be death!" As she spoke these words, she drew a dagger from her belt and pointed it to her breast. "Spurn my love," she said, "and this weapon will enter my heart! I will not live without thee; but if I die, my death will also cost thee thy life; for if my body is found in this grotto to-morrow, thou wilt be accused of being my murderer, and be executed for it." Seeing that her threats had no effect upon the Neophyte, she threw the dagger upon the floor, and, sinking down at his feet, implored him for his love. She tore away her veil, and her beautiful hair dropped over her shoulders; tears streamed from her eyes, and her appeals ended in sobs.

"Depart!" sternly answered Jesus, and the fair one arose and retreated; but as she disappeared from sight, another door opened, and a stream of light entered the room. The Hierophant and some of the Brothers appeared at the entrance, and, congratulating him on his victory which he had gained, they led him to a large hall, where, after submitting to the ceremony of baptism, he was pronounced to be worthy to be admitted to a higher degree.

Thus should he, who is the guardian of the door, beware that no secret entrance is left open, by which a favorite passion may enter, and if the temptress should enter unaware, during his slumber, he should call to his aid the superior power of his awakened Will, and repel her. Then will the door of his soul be open, Reason will enter and guide him by the light of Divine Wisdom nearer to permanent Peace.

"To learn the mysteries of the Spirit, we must descend into the subterranean caves where the treasures are hidden."

'ter a few days of rest and contemplation, Jesus

was told that the time had arrived when his courage
and daring would have to undergo a severe trial.
IIis eyes were again blindfolded, and he was taken
to a subterranean cave, into which he had to descend
by means of a ladder.   Having arrived at the bottom, he removed the bandage from his eyes, according to the directions he had previously received; but
he could see no light.   The cavern was dark, and at
first he could not discern any objects; but he heard
hissing sounds close by his side.   He made a few
steps in advance, and stepped upon a living thing
that was gliding over the floor, and which immediately wriggled itself around his leg.   Then the fact
immediately came to his consciousness that he was
in a den of serpents, and that to faint would mean
to be lost.   Gradually his eyes became accustomed to
the deep darkness, and he discerned the eyes and
forms of the reptiles that lurked in all the corners.
The cavern seemed to be filled with snakes of all
kinds.   Twisted together in disgusting knots, some
were lying on the floor, and others wormed themselves over the rocks.   He seated himself upon a
stone, and soon the snakes began to approach, as if to
resent his presence.   They crawled over his legs,
twisted themselves around his arms and all over his
body.

At first Jesus was horrified; but his horror was
only of a moment's duration, for he immediately
called to his aid his higher consciousness and re-
membered that his terrestrial form, subject to the
disgusting embraces of the crawling reptiles, and
made of the same stuff as they, was not his real Self,
but merely a form to which he—the divine Man—

was for the time being attached. This thought enabled him to look upon everything that might happen to his body as if he were an independent spectator. In this way he appealed for aid to his own God, and as he did so, a superior strength, a power unknown before, seemed to pervade his whole body, and now it seemed as if his power had invested him with some property that made him repulsive to the serpents; for soon the reptiles that were in contact with his body left him and retired into their holes.

Thus if man descends to the innermost depths of his soul, he may find it infested with poisonous serpents and venomous reptiles, the symbols of the brood of passions and spirit of evil desires; but if he calls to his aid the divine Wisdom, the persecutions will cease and peace will return.

After having passed through this severe trial, he was released from his prison and led again to the temple.

For a second time his spiritual eyes were opened by the Magic power of the Hierophant, and he was made to behold in his vision a *Griffin* and a *turning wheel with four spokes.* Then the whole process of Evolution became clear to his understanding, and he saw how in the course of millions of ages, worlds upon worlds had been evolved from the incomprehensible *centre.* He beheld waves of Life passing from planet to planet, and each fiery orb, each globe, each solar system, had peculiar forms of its own, and all these various forms were manifestations of one and the same Supreme Power, that men call "God," and formed out of its own substance.

The air, the earth, and the water were filled with

forms of life, having bodies of a kind of manner too refined to be seen by mortal eyes. Some were luminous, others dark, and the regions above the sphere of the Earth were inhabited by beings of a seemingly supernatural beauty. He saw the *Nature-spirits* of the four elements. He saw what Man had been in the distant past and what he would be at a future period of time far beyond the calculation of mortals. He saw how the gross material elements of which the Earth is now composed, would in the far-distant future be changed into a substance of a superior and ethereal kind, so that what we now call "Earth" would be like water, and what we call "Water" like air, and what we call "Air" like the ether of space, and with the transformation of all beings, Man himself would enter into a superior state of existence.

The science which deals with these problems is far too grand and extensive to be more than merely touched upon in these pages, nor would it benefit the uninitiated reader, if we were to enter into its details; for so long as the *interior* perception which enables men to perceive these things is not opened, such a discussion will be a mere matter of speculation, serving more for amusement than for the attainment of knowledge.

In this degree he was taught the great law of *Karma;* that is to say, the law of Cause and Effect, not merely upon the physical plane, where the law of *Mechanics* exists, but in that higher realm, where divine *Justice* rules supreme, where Good finds its own reward, and Evil its own punishment. He saw that whatever man may think or do, would produce a corresponding reaction upon himself, and that he who

benefits others is thereby benefiting himself, while he
who injures others is thereby decreeing his own punishment. He saw that the acts of men are the external symbols of their *interior* lives, and that every
thought and act has a tendency to repeat itself.
Thoughts seemed to him like beings struggling for
life, seeking to become embodied in acts; and if they
were once thus embodied, they clung to their life in
the same way as man clings to his, but the power
which invested these thoughts with life was the Will,
and unless man's thoughts were kept alive by his
Will, they died and putrefied like the corporeal
things upon the physical plane.*

The length of the time during which the *Necoris*
had to remain in the second degree, before he was
permitted to enter the third, called *Melanephores*, de-
pended on his own progress. Many never attained
any higher than the second degree; but those who
were permitted to advance higher had to pass through
the *Portal of Death;* for this was the name of the
door through which they who desired to obtain powers which belong to a higher than merely personal
existence had to enter, before they could acquire
them.

Without hesitation Jesus followed those who were
appointed to guide him. They descended into the
tombs, where the mummies were kept and which
were to be a living tomb to him, if he did not succeed
in liberating himself therefrom by his own magic
power. The room which he entered was filled with

---

* See the secret instructions concerning the *Elementals*
in "The Beautiful Philosophy of Initiation."

16 1

corpses of the dead, while in the midst of the chamber stood the sarcophagus of *osiris* still overflowing with blood.   The *Paraskites*—i. e., the men who opened the bodies of the dead—and the *Heroi*—who attended to the embalming—were at their work. From thence he entered into another room, where he was met by all the *Melanephores*, dressed in black. They took him before the *King*, and the latter addressing him in a very kind manner, advised him to desist from further attempts to penetrate still deeper into the Mysteries, and to remain satisfied with that which he had already gained.   He praised the Neophyte for his courage and virtues and told him that it were better for him to remain contented and to desist from further research.   He told him that if he would do so, he would be highly honored by all on account of the knowledge he had already gained; and in token of the high esteem in which he held the Neophyte, the king took his own golden crown from his head and offered it to him.   But Jesus, understanding the meaning of the symbol, threw the crown down upon the floor and stepped upon it with his foot, saying that it was not his object to be admired and to gratify his ambition for fame or to be praised by men; but that he desired wisdom and desired it for its own sake alone.

As he did so, a cry of indignation arose from those present and a ceremony took place which upon the external plane represented the well-known *internal truth, that Ambition is the King of all passions and that to give up one's Ambition is like giving up one's own self; for man's soul being made up to a great extent of desires, dies the mystic death, when he kills his ruling desire. It is then "as if the heart were bleeding and the whole life of man seems to be utterly dissolved."*

This was the terrible ordeal through which Jesus had to pass, and through which every other Neophyte must pass if he desires Initiation, and before he can enter the Temple of Wisdom.

The judgment of the departed soul before *Pluto, Rhadamantes,* and *Minos* was then enacted; for when the king of *ambition* in the soul of man dies, his daughter, *Vanity,* dies with him, and in his place arises a sense of one's unworthiness. The *accusing, judging,* and *revenging* angels then appear in the soul, until the tortured heart sends its despairing cries to the *Redeemer,* the *Truth;* when the celestial *powers awaken within,* to comfort the soul and guide her to the harbor of *peace.*

During this process of ceremony the whole of Jesus's past life, with all the minutest details that ever took place *within* his mental organization, appeared before his vision; but when the initiation was ended he knew that the *lower* elements *within* his soul had died and that he himself had been changed into another being. He then received the special instructions belonging to this degree, and he was especially shown the sanctity of all life and the full meaning of the words: *"Thou shalt not kill."*

While he remained in this degree, the *Hierogram-matical* art of writing, the history of Egypt, geography, cosmology, and astronomy were taught him; *but his principal occupation, in this as in all other degrees, was the cultivation of the power of Intuition, by which man may know the truth and attain wis-*

*dom, independent of all books or external informa-
tion and without the necessity of adopting the opinions of others.*

For a long time Jesus remained in the tombs, at-
tending to the disposal of the bodies of the dead;
nor was any one of the members of this degree ever
permitted to leave them during the rest of their natural lives, unless they attained that Magic Power,
known to the *Adept,* by which the Astral body of man
may leave at will the prison house of the terrestrial
body. Those who were not able to acquire this power
had to remain in their tombs, and their duty was to
attend to the embalming and the burial of the dead.

*Thus the souls of those who are incapable of enter-
ing a higher state of consciousness during their terrestrial lives, will have to remain within their living
tombs of gross matter, overshadowed by the darkness of ignorance, engaged in ministering to that
which is worthless and without eternal life, and to
preserve from decay useless memories of terrestrial
things. They will continue to follow their worthless occupations and be servants of empty forms and
illusions until the angel of death releases them from
their prisons, to lead them from the darkness of
matter into the eternal darkness beyond.*

"He who thoroughly knows his own self, knows everything."

"The fourth degree of the Essenian Brotherhood
was called *'The Battles of the Shadows.'* In this
degree the Christophores (Christos) — as he was now
called — was taught the nature of *Good* and *Evil* and
how to conquer Evil by Good. He was taught how
to cut off the head of the beautiful *Gorgon,* without

hesitating on account of her almost supernaturally beautiful form. He was instructed in the art of *Necromancy, i. e.,* the art to deal with the *astral bodies* of the dead and with those dangerous beings, called *Elementals,** who inhabited the *astral world,* and to make them subservient to their will. Woe to him whom the power of spiritual Will deserted even for one moment during these trials; the principles of Evil which he attempted to subject to his Will would then become his masters, and insanity or death was the result.

In attempting to describe some of the mysteries of the Higher Degrees in the Essenian Brotherhood, we are attempting to enter upon a field where only those can enter who have themselves obtained some experience of practical Occultism; for how could the *magic* processes that took place in the *"Battle of the Shadows"* be described to persons whose knowledge consists merely of the information they have received from an age which denies that magic or spiritual powers exist? It will require perhaps centuries of scientific investigation before our sceptics will understand the Magic power of the *spiritually awakened Will,* and before they can be brought to a knowledge that feats of Magic do not belong to the realm of the fable, and it may require many centuries more, before such powers will become the property of the many.

And yet the world is still full of Magic. The magic power of *Love* still exercises its influence over the hearts; the magic of *Imagination* still makes

---

* See the "Beautiful Philosophy of Initiation."

men mournful or glad; the *Will* of the strong still
controls by its magic power the mind of the weak,
and the foolish are still ruled by the superior magic
power of the spirit of those who are wise; but such
wonders like that of the growth of a tree, do not surprise us, merely because we are accustomed to witness them every day.

The Egyptian Adepts and Magicians may not have
been in possession of all that our modern science
knows in regard to the relations which exist between
external phenomena; but they had a method, *known
only to a few of our present age,* to develop the power
to look into that realm called the invisible, but which
is a world far more real and substantial than the so-
called visible world.   Men are prone to jump at conclusions drawn from sensual observation and to regard the visible side of nature as the actual world
and to reject that which is beyond sensual perception; but even a superficial reflection will convince
man that the terms "visible" and invisible" are merely *relative;* for whether or not a thing may be seen
by us, depends not merely on its own nature, but
also on the construction and quality of the organs of
our perception.   What may be seen by one, may be
invisible to another who is devoid of the organ of
sight; and what may be invisible to many, may be
visible to those whose *inner* powers of perception
have become open.

*There is no relative Good without relative Evil.
There is no man so pure, as not to have some animal
elements within his constitution, and were there such
a man, he would not be able to develop higher; for
it is this very animal element from which the soul*

of man draws its nourishment and strength to rise
higher and to become more spiritual. Not to destroy,
but to make use of the elements of evil in man for
the purpose of accomplishing good, is the object of
the higher education. When the higher life begins to
awaken within the soul and the light of the Spirit
penetrates into the regions of the elementals, the animal egoes begin to revolt and to rise to the surface.
They may even appear in objective form and persecute their creator. Then the dread dweller of the
threshhold may show his face. He is nothing else but
a product of man's own imagination, but nevertheless
living and as real as any other living thing among
the so-called realities of this world, and if the candidate for Initiation is subject to fear, he may become its victim and insanity result, for the Dweller
of the Threshold will then again and with increased
power take possession of his mind.*

There is a region in the soul of man in which such
Dwellers reside. In very degraded persons this region swarms with living, semi-developed or full-
grown animal principles and subjective monstrosities
of all kinds and under certain conditions, especially
if the physical organism is weakened by disease, they
may—so to say—step out of their centre, and assume
an objective form, clothing themselves in the grosser
elements of matter and becoming visible even to the
external senses. The Materialization of modern
Spiritualism furnishes an example of this.

If the candidate in that Brotherhood succeeded in

---

* See "History of the Rosicrucians," and "Beautiful Philosophy of Initiation."

overcoming all these obstacles, he became a partaker of the *Demiurgos*—the creative power in nature, and in possession of absolute Truth. The *bitter cup* which he was to drink, caused him to rise above all earthly ills arising from his lower nature, and he received his daily food from the *King*. His name was then entered into the *Book of Life—Immortality,* and he became one of the *judges of the country.* His emblem was an *Owl*, representing *Isis*, the Goddess of Nature; he was presented with a *palm leaf* and an *olive branch*, the emblems of *Peace*. The "password" of that degree was *ioa*—Jehovah, and the understanding of its exoteric signification involved a knowledge of the creative principle in Nature. Henceforth he received his instructions from no man, but from the *Demiurgic*—Spiritually Awakened— *Mind*.

He who had attended the degree of *Christophores* was entitled to apply to the *Demiurgos* for the still higher degree of *Balahate*. In this degree he was permitted to see *Typhoon*—Divinity in his terrible form; of endless extent, containing within himself all that exists in the Universe; the All-creator and All-destroyer.

"With eyes and faces, infinite in form,
   The everlasting Cause, a mass of Light,
In every region hard to look upon;
   Bright as the blaze of the burning fire and sun,
On every side, and vast beyond all bounds."
                        —*Bhagavad Gita.*

But the *Balahate* had awakeend to a full consciousness of the Immortal principle *within*, and was no longer terrified to see the destruction of all changeable things. He now knew the nature of the *secret fire* that regenerates the world and which renders him who comes into its possession immortal.

In the sixth degree the Adept was instructed by the Demiurgos in all the secrets of *Astrology;* that is to say, in the science of the spiritual aspects of the stars; he learned to know the directions of the spiritual life-currents, pervading the *Soul of the Universe;* he became even a being superior to the *Devas* and *Angels* and in possession of all spiritual powers.

The seventh and highest degree, called *Pahcha,* could not be applied for, but was conferred by the power of divine *Grace* upon those who were willing to receive it. In this divine degree, the holiest of holies, the ultimate mystery was revealed to the spiritual perception of the Adept. He received a *Cross,* which he had to wear continually during his terrestrial life, the hair upon his head was cut off, he received the key to the understanding of all the Mysteries, he obtained the privilege to elect the king of the country, or—to speak in plain words and leave off allegorical expressions—*his soul became one with the ruler of all and he entered into the essence of God.*"

Whether the events described in these pages ever took place on the *external* or on the *internal* plane, or on *both,* the reader may decide for himself. If such things are enacted merely externally without taking place internally, then they are mere shams. Every external act which is not true representation of internal life is a sham, and our modern civilization is made up of such shams. Our secret societies have come into possession of some of the forms and ceremonies used by the Ancient Egyptians; but they have merely the *form;* the spirit went away long ago. *Let him who would follow the path of true Initiation remember this, that, if he desires to reach and become an Initiate he must follow the Path so plainly laid out.*

First comes *thought,* and afterwards comes that *interior Illumination* by which men are baptized with *fire* from the Holy Spirit of Truth, that descends upon those who are pure in heart, like a white dove descending from heaven. Man may be led up to the truth by argumentation, but he can only be saved by knowledge. Reason is the prophet, but Wisdom is the Redeemer. Thought must precede knowledge; but without the Light of Divine Wisdom thought is like a voice in the wilderness, calling for help; an intellect without Love becomes easily lost in the mazes of speculations and misleading opinions. Therefore you, who desire to be saved, repent of your errors; give up your selfishness, that causes you to seek for knowledge *merely* on account of the benefits you hope to derive therefrom; open your eyes to see the true saviour, the Light of Wisdom, which you may find below the dark clouds of ignorance by which your heart is surrounded."

THE END.